An Architect's Guide to

NEC3

An Architect's Guide to

NEC3

RIBA Publishing

Frances Forward

© Frances Forward, 2011

Published by RIBA Publishing,
15 Bonhill Street, London EC2P 2EA

ISBN 978 1 85946 351 2
Stock code 69975

The right of Frances Forward to be identified as the Author of this Work
has been asserted in accordance with the Copyright, Designs and
Patents Act 1988.

British Library Cataloguing in Publications Data
A catalogue record for this book is available from the British Library.

Commissioning Editor: James Thompson
Project Editor: Alasdair Deas
Designed and typeset by Liaison Design
Printed and bound by Charlesworth

Photographs (pages x-xi)
1: Richard Learoyd. 2, 4: London 2012. 3: Steve Taylor. 5: Halley VI,
designed by Hugh Broughton Architects and AECOM and constructed
by Galliford Try International for the British Antarctic Survey. Image by 7-t.

RIBA Publishing is part of RIBA Enterprises Ltd.
www.ribaenterprises.com

Foreword

In my *Constructing the Team* report of 1994 I commented 'if the NEC becomes normal construction contract documentation', which could be taken as my prediction of what may happen if my recommendations were followed through. I recommended that 'use of the NEC to increase' with the action by client bodies including the Department of the Environment in conjunction with other government departments, this action to take place 'as soon as possible'. I went on to recommend a target be set of 'one third of Government funded projects started over the next four years to use the NEC' and that 'use of the NEC (as amended) by private sector clients should be strongly promoted by client and industry bodies'. I highlighted what I considered constituted a modern contract, commenting that 'The New Engineering Contract contains virtually all of these assumptions of best practice, and others, which are set out in the Core Clauses, the main and secondary options'. I further commented that a 'full matrix of consultants' and adjudicators' terms of appointment should be published, interlocked with the main contract', and that 'provision should be made for a simpler and shorter minor works document'.

NEC has come a long way since these thoughts and recommendations were laid down in my report. It was then a single contract called the New Engineering Contract, a contract between an Employer and a Contractor, for construction and engineering works. As the family grew, New Engineering Contract became the name of the family of standard contracts in 1995, each contract having its own name, such as Engineering and Construction Contract, Engineering and Construction Subcontract and Engineering and Construction Short Contract. The family name was then shortened to NEC3 in 2005, with the '3' signifying the third generation launch of this suite of documents. The suite includes contracts, guidance notes and flow charts, and now provides contracts for the procurement of goods, works and services. We now have the full matrix, interlocking with the main contract, as well as having the shorter minor works contract I felt was needed. In fact, the family has grown well beyond my and most people's expectations from its early conceptual stages.

My targets for use by government-funded projects didn't meet the timescales, but NEC3 contracts are now significantly used by government departments. This is no doubt also aided by the Office of Government Commerce's decision in 2005 to endorse NEC3 contracts for use in the UK public sector.

NEC now has international coverage and, I am advised, has been used in around 30 countries to date, including very considerable use in South Africa and New Zealand. The upward trend is not only a testimony to the quality and content of the NEC3 contracts, but also a recognition that it both helps produce the parties' desired results and contains processes that clients and their supply chains require to meet their modern ways of doing business. Adversarialism is replaced with mutual trust and co-operation; hindsight with foresight; reactive behaviour with proactivity. We are part way there, but there is still much to do!

Use of the NEC continues to grow and it is being used on most major UK projects along the way. Channel Tunnel Rail Link, Heathrow Terminal 5 and the 2012 Olympics are but a few examples, Crossrail being the latest mega-project to use NEC. It is pleasing to note that very little case law has come from NEC contracts and let us hope this continues.

On to this publication, I was pleased to provide the foreword to Frances for *An Architect's Guide to NEC3*. I hope that architects see the benefits that the NEC system can bring to a project as well as appreciating the key role an architect plays in this.

Sir Michael Latham

About the author

Frances Forward BA(Hons) Dip Arch MSc(Const Law) RIBA FCIArb is a practising architect, adjudicator and lecturer with extensive experience in design, management and consulting roles within the construction industry, both in the UK and in Germany. Frances' Master's research in the early 1990s into a potential European standard form construction contract led her to explore the genesis of the fledging NEC contract and she went on to pioneer the use of the NEC on complex lottery-funded arts projects.

Frances set up her own architectural practice in 1999 and the NEC became her contract of choice, for both professional services and construction. In 2000, Frances was invited to assist the NEC Panel in drafting the NEC Partnering Option X12 and she subsequently became the architect member of the Panel during the drafting of the third edition, NEC3.

Frances expanded her architectural practice in 2005 to offer an additional role of management contractor, in order to allow clients to procure both the design, and the off-site fabrication plus on-site construction of sustainable buildings from a single company. The partnering supply chain for her company includes both English and German specialist subconsultants and subcontractors, using NEC3 as the common form of contract.

Frances has contributed to a number of publications and conferences regarding the NEC and she lectures on the NEC at various university schools of architecture as part of their professional practice programmes.

Contents

The widely differing building projects shown here have all been procured under NEC3 contracts, demonstrating NEC3's inherent flexibility – creative designs deserve a creative contract.

1 Centre for Mathematical Sciences, Cambridge University *Edward Cullinan Architects*

2 London 2012 Olympics, Aquatics Centre *Zaha Hadid Architects*

3 Residential building, Winchester *Haus Ltd Architects*

4 London 2012 Olympics, Olympic Village Plot 7: *Glenn Howells Architects*

5 Halley VI Antarctic Research Station *Hugh Broughton Architects*

Introduction

Over two decades, the NEC has evolved from a 'revolutionary' new form of contract to become a mainstream standard form contract which is particularly conducive to collaborative working and contractual partnering. Use of the NEC has grown steadily in all sectors of the construction industry over its lifetime and a working knowledge of it has become essential for all architects, allied professionals, clients and contractors involved in building projects. Following the OGC[1] endorsement of NEC3 on its publication in 2005, the use of any other form of construction contract on publicly procured projects has declined to a point where no one involved in such work can afford to be ignorant of NEC3. Use of the NEC is increasingly driven by client bodies and while architects in some specialist building sectors – such as healthcare and transport – are relatively conversant with the NEC, other architects have limited awareness of it. Architects are also increasingly exposed to the NEC in the private sector and need to be comfortable with it in relation to all potential projects.

The RIBA Plan of Work and architectural education at Part 3 level acknowledge that architects give procurement advice; in practice, a lack of consistent knowledge about the NEC among the architectural profession could put architects at risk of giving incomplete procurement advice. The key aim of this book is to make an adequate level of knowledge readily available to all architects. The book is intended to make NEC3 more accessible to many and at many levels.

Given the legacy of the Victorian era in the evolution of older style standard form construction contracts, there is particular need for all professionals to look very clearly at the provisions of NEC3 as a modern standard form contract, capable of supporting best practice in project management. Furthermore, given the historical divergence of the building and engineering sectors of the construction industry in the UK, there is also a particular need to distinguish the specific relevance of the multidisciplinary NEC3 contract to building sector professionals.

A number of books have been written on various aspects and uses of the NEC contract, encompassing its multidisciplinary nature; however, these have tended to focus on its use primarily in the engineering sector of the construction industry and on its legal interpretation. This is the first book to date to focus in detail on the specific needs of the building sector within the construction industry and consequently sets the NEC3 scene in the context of an architect's perspective and professional responsibilities.

1. Office of Government Commerce.

1 Background to the NEC

Procurement strategy

Contract typology

Conventionally, the parameters of time, cost and quality have been assessed in relation to choosing the correct type of contract for individual projects on the following basis:

- **time:** design and construction duration *and* certainty of end date

- **cost:** overall price (fees and construction) *and* certainty of final account

- **quality:** specification standards *and* workmanship on-site.

The procurement analysis of the relative importance of time, cost and quality has historically led to a decision as to whether a traditional, a design and build or a management procurement route is appropriate. However, such analysis has also long been predicated on the convention that time will be somewhat compromised under traditional procurement routes, quality will be somewhat compromised under design and build procurement routes and cost will be somewhat compromised under management procurement routes. The arguments leading to this convention are well rehearsed and need not be examined in detail here, as their only real relevance in the context of the NEC is that they represent an outmoded and arguably superseded approach to procurement strategy.

A further subset of contract typology is the payment mechanism, which conventionally includes the following categories:

- lump sum

- remeasurement

- cost reimbursable.

These generic payment mechanisms remain relevant in the context of the NEC, albeit the NEC offers greater sophistication in their implementation than earlier standard form contracts.

It should be noted that no type of standard form contract, including NEC3, offers either a 'fixed price' or a 'guaranteed maximum price' payment mechanism, these being inventions of those who seek to amend standard form contracts or draft bespoke contracts to highly polarise risk allocation.

Contract form

Professional drafting bodies historically published standard form contracts based on traditional procurement strategy[2] and subsequently responded to analysis of the so-called 'time/cost/quality triangle' by publishing additional design and build and management versions of their standard forms. Architects have long been used to providing clients with procurement advice, and indeed are expected to advise on both the 'Identification of procurement method'[3] and the 'Review of procurement route'[4] at a relatively early stage in a project. While this is an important advisory role, there seems to be a need for flexibility and further review.

---

2. I.e. the separation of design and construction.
3. RIBA Outline Plan of Work 2007 (amended November 2008/January 2009): Work Stage B.
4. Ibid.: Work Stage C.

Project-specific strategies

Increasingly, a need has developed for contracts to respond to individual project requirements in a more finely calibrated manner; project sponsors simply can no longer accept that only two-and-a-half out of the three parameters of time, cost and quality are adequately controlled. The resultant requirement for project-specific procurement strategies leads to what might be described as a hybrid procurement route. Such a route inevitably calls for much more flexible contracts than conventional procurement routes do, which might partly explain the apparent growth in the drafting of entirely bespoke construction contracts for important projects.

There is arguably a fourth procurement parameter that most twenty-first century construction projects require to be taken account of and that is risk. NEC3 sets out to offer a highly flexible format, which responds to the prototype nature of many construction projects and provides the ability to build up an appropriate contract. NEC3 enables a breakaway from conventional procurement analysis with no necessary compromise between time, cost, quality or risk management.

Genesis and philosophy of the NEC

Origins

The genesis of the NEC[5] was an initiative in the mid-1980s by a new Legal Affairs Committee within the ICE[6] in London. This initiative resulted primarily from a general dissatisfaction with Victorian-style standard form contracts within the construction industry, which had been conceived of prior to the commonplace requirement for complex multidisciplinary projects and which had become increasingly convoluted, in response to the perception of a 'high risk' and 'adversarial' construction industry. The initial strategy for a 'modern' contract was developed by a small team led by Dr Martin Barnes[7] and a consultative version of the NEC was published in 1991; this was generally received with such enthusiasm that it was followed by an official first edition in 1993. The NEC received important endorsement in the UK Government/industry Latham Report[8] of 1994 and the NEC second edition was published in 1995. The partnering ethos of the NEC contract was further endorsed in the UK Government/industry Egan Report[9] of 1998. A review of the NEC in use and users' comments was undertaken by its drafting panel, under the auspices of its publisher[10] and the third edition, NEC3, was published in 2005.

Application – what's in a name?

An important factor in the interest generated in the NEC was its applicability to a very broad range of 'engineering' projects. This was officially extended to include all construction projects following the Latham Report, although the revised title 'Engineering and Construction Contract' (ECC) – intended to emphasise the contract's wide range of applicability – never really captured end users' imagination and the original name NEC largely prevailed. Ironically, architects' initial interest in the NEC might have been greatly increased and subsequent interest accelerated had the title been revised to 'Engineering and Building Contract'. The answer to 'what's in a name?' in this instance seems to be 'quite a lot'!

---

5. New Engineering Contract.
6. Institution of Civil Engineers.
7. BSc(Eng) PhD FICE FCIOB FAPM FICES MBCS CCMI FREng CBE.
8. Latham, M. (1994) *Constructing the Team*, London: HMSO.
9. Egan, J. (1998) *Rethinking Construction: Report of the Construction Task Force*, London: HMSO.
10. Thomas Telford Publishing, London.

There was also a clear intention that the NEC should be conceived as a contract that would be operable globally (see Chapter 5) and the drafting is intended to facilitate diversity on a number of levels.

Guiding principles

The approach to the design of the NEC encompassed the concept that both the legal and the management requirements of a diverse range of modern projects could be met in a single document and that the avoidance of legalistic language would assist in that aim.

The principles of risk theory and risk management were also important considerations and an early decision was made that the contracting parties and their representatives should be required to act in a 'spirit of mutual trust and co-operation'.[11]

The stated objectives of the NEC[12] are *flexibility, clarity* and *simplicity*, as well as providing a *stimulus to good management*. In practice, the NEC approach offers a range of benefits that are key to its success:

- 'pick and mix' contract conditions, to suit both the project and the project team

- plain English, giving both legal and project management rights and obligations equal status

- real-time project management, with contemporaneous decision-making, and

- cross-industry application, facilitating multidisciplinary working practices.[13]

The NEC3 contract family

The NEC3 family relationship for architects

It is pertinent to emphasise that the NEC has been designed for extremely flexible use patterns; different family members will therefore have different levels of significance for users, depending on each user's discipline. Architects will tend to be interested in all the family members (Figure 1); however, they are likely to have the closest relationship with the *Black Book* and the NEC3 Short Contract in the context of building contracts, and with the *Orange Book* in the context of professional services.

The NEC3 Subcontract and the NEC3 Short Subcontract will also be significant for architects in the context of specialist design and installation. Historically, architects have tended to take much less notice of subcontract conditions than main contract conditions, often believing the detail of them to be a contractor's responsibility and largely outside the sphere of an architect's influence. Given the decline in direct employment of staff by contractors and the greater reliance on specialist subcontractors to realise projects, architects who ignore subcontract conditions may do so at their peril. A number of drafting bodies have attempted to improve co-ordination between main contracts and subcontracts; however, NEC contracts have been at the forefront of a co-ordinated approach since their inception.

---

11. Core clause 10.1.
12. NEC3 Guidance Notes, June 2005.
13. Envisaged in the Banwell Report, 1964.

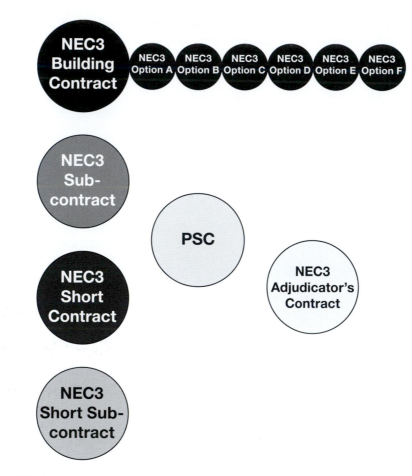

Figure 1   NEC3 'immediate' family: building projects

Compatibility, 'nesting' of contracts and uniformity

The risk of incompatible rights and obligations as between Employer and Contractor within the building contract or as between Employer and Consultants within their respective professional services contracts is greatly reduced with the provision for back-to-back contractual arrangements. The risk of incompatible obligations as between Contractor and Subcontractor is similarly reduced. The back-to-back drafting has the further benefit that there is no necessary connection between the status of the parties and the type of contract to be entered into, as between construction and professional services.

It is possible to 'nest' a number of contracts within each other, irrespective of whether the head contract is for construction or professional services. The conventional approach may be perceived as nesting subcontracts into a construction contract – or in the context of design and build procurement, also nesting professional services contracts into a construction contract. However, the flexibility of the NEC allows not only for the nesting of 'same' contracts within each other (e.g. NEC3 Subcontracts or NEC3 Professional Services Contracts), but also potentially for unconventional nesting, such as construction within professional services.

To encourage uniform application of the NEC methodology, comprehensive Guidance Notes and logical Flow Charts are published in parallel with each of the NEC3 contract versions, as well as guidance on Procurement and Contract Strategies. These do not form part of the contract itself, but nevertheless provide valuable assistance in understanding and operating the project management principles of the contract. Architects may find the Flow Charts particularly useful in operating NEC3 contracts, as the graphic representation and proven functionality encourage a rigorous and yet creative approach to project management.

NEC3 published contracts

Generally, there has been an attempt to provide as few separate contracts as possible, preferring the 'pick and mix' approach, although some separation has proved desirable. All previously published NEC contracts were revised in 2005 as the third edition and all new NEC contracts published since 2005 are also classified as NEC3 for consistency.

In order of their importance to architects, the NEC3 family comprises the following publications.

The NEC3 'Building' (Engineering and Construction) Contract
(June 2005)

The so-called *'Black Book'*

Architects could be forgiven for unofficially renaming this the NEC3 'building' Contract. It is very important for architects to bear in mind that this single book represents a standard form building contract blueprint, which is equally appropriate for traditional, design and build, management and hybrid procurements strategies. It is this universality that is of paramount importance in giving architects and their clients real choice, both at the outset of projects and, where necessary, during later stages of the procurement process.

The NEC3 'building' Contract is also published individually for each of the six 'payment mechanism' main options – Options A to F (see *Main option clauses*, page 20) – although this is for convenience, not necessity, and should certainly not be misunderstood, in that it remains a single contract form.

The NEC3 Short Contract
(June 2005)

(Blue Book)

Building clients may find this version of NEC3 appropriate where the project is relatively straightforward, without the need for much fine-tuning of the contract conditions (see *Secondary option clauses*, page 32). The Employer and the Contractor communicate directly with one another, without a dedicated 'contract administrator', although there is provision for 'delegated authority' from the Employer. Perhaps the most helpful way of deciding whether the NEC3 Short Contract might be appropriate is to consider it to be suitable for low-complexity projects, rather than low-value projects. Historically, some standard form drafting bodies have made minor works contracts available and indicated that they are suitable for contracts up to certain (relatively low) monetary values. The critical point with the NEC3 Short Contract is that it may be eminently suitable for high-value contracts, provided that the work content of such contracts is relatively simple.

The NEC3 Subcontract
(June 2005)

The so-called *'Purple Book'*

It is no exaggeration to state that the only significant difference between the *Purple Book* and the *Black Book* is simply that the *Purple Book* refers to the Contractor rather than the Employer, and to the Subcontractor rather than the Contractor. However, this deceptively simple swap is in turn the key to the success of the NEC3 Subcontract – it is genuinely back-to-back with the *Black Book* (see *Subcontracting*, page 63).

The NEC3 Short Subcontract
(June 2005)

(Turquoise Book)

In a mirror of the *Purple Book–Black Book* relationship, it is also no exaggeration to state that the only significant difference between the NEC3 Short Subcontract and the NEC3 Short Contract is simply that the Short Subcontract refers to the Contractor rather than the Employer and to the Subcontractor rather than the Contractor. The Short Subcontract is therefore not only genuinely back-to-back with the Subcontract, but also offers an alternative to the *Purple Book* for works of a simple nature to be subcontracted under the *Black Book*.

The NEC3 Professional Services Contract (PSC)
(June 2005)

The so-called *'Orange Book'*

The PSC (see *Professional services*, page 59) is interesting for architects in that, like the NEC3 Subcontract, it offers the potential for back-to-back contractual arrangements. This potential may be particularly relevant where architects are employed initially by clients and subsequently by contractors under design and build procurement arrangements, in that there is likely to be much less potential for disparity between pre- and post-novation obligations. Another context in which the back-to-back potential is likely to assist architects is where they are involved in projects side-by-side with a number of other specialist consultants; whether the architects are acting as lead consultant or not, there will be much less risk of gaps and/or overlaps in the totality of the consultants' work.

The NEC3 Adjudicator's Contract
(June 2005)

(Green Book)

The adjudicator has had a role under the NEC Contract since prior to the introduction of statutory adjudication in England and Wales.[14] It has always been considered advantageous to treat the adjudicator, as a person involved in a project, in a potentially positive way from the outset. The corollary to this perspective is that an NEC adjudicator should be signed up from the beginning; this is the basis upon which the NEC3 Adjudicator's Contract is intended to operate (see *Dispute management*, page 56).

The NEC3 Term Service Contract (TSC)
(June 2005)

(Grey Book)

Essentially, the TSC (see *Partnering,* page 64 and *Framework agreements*, page 68) is intended to operate with the same flexibility and control as the *Black Book* but for ongoing works, such as maintenance tasks, which cannot be fully defined from the outset.

The NEC3 Framework Contract
(June 2005)

(Beige Book)

The NEC3 Framework Contract (see *Framework agreements*, page 68) provides a standard umbrella contract for other NEC3 contracts to be potentially instructed to prequalified suppliers[15] over a set period. Architects working in the context of public procurement[16] may find the NEC3 Framework Contract a valuable addition to the NEC contract family, in that it will obviate the need for bespoke framework contracts, which can often be in conflict with the terms of standard form contracts under them.

The NEC3 Term Service Short Contract (TSSC)
(September 2008)

(Aubergine Book)

The NEC3 Term Service Short Contract (TSSC) offers a simple methodology for ongoing maintenance-type works of a straightforward nature. The Employer and the Contractor communicate directly with one another, without a dedicated contract administrator, although the contract provides the option of the Employer appointing an Employer's Agent.

---

14. Housing Grants Construction and Regeneration Act (HGCR Act) 1996 brought into force with The Scheme for Construction Contracts (England and Wales) Regulations on 1 May 1998.
15. Whether Consultants or Contractors.
16. Within the European Union.

The NEC3 Supply Contract

(December 2009)

(Red Book)

The NEC3 Supply Contract is intended for the purchase (locally or internationally) of high-value goods and related services, which may include design.

The NEC3 Supply Short Contract

(December 2009)

(Brown Book)

The NEC3 Supply Short Contract is intended for the purchase of relatively simple goods.

2 Structure and content of NEC3

'Pick and mix' assembly of the contract

Clause hierarchy and contract layout

Of paramount importance is that the NEC3 contract conditions are structured as a three-tier shopping list, comprising (1) core clauses, (2) main option clauses and (3) secondary option clauses, from which the necessary items must be selected (Figure 2). The selection criteria are to be found in the project type and risk profile.

A fundamental drafting decision, which has been key to the clarity of the NEC clauses in practice, was to take advantage of starting from the beginning and to arrange the document in a logical order. First, there is a clear group of concepts set out in nine *core clause* sections and, therein, a clear sequence of clauses dealing with the specific nature of each concept. Cross-referencing between clauses is avoided and related elements are kept within the individual sections. The drafting of these core clause sections is genuinely generic, with the clear intention that they are applicable to any project, whatever its nature, wherever it is in the world and under whatever jurisdiction. Second, there are six *main options*, of which one main option is chosen to determine the pricing mechanism applicable to a particular project; each main option adds the clauses required to operate that particular pricing mechanism. Third, there is a series of *secondary option* clauses to assist in fine-tuning the contract to meet the specific needs of the project; an assessment is made as to which, if any, of these secondary option clauses should be selected to meet the specific needs of the project. Finally, a decision is made as to which *dispute resolution option* applies.

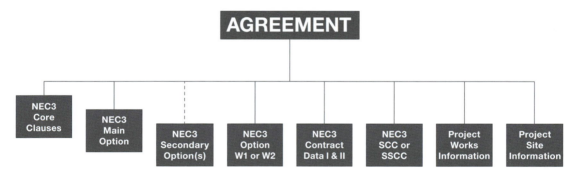

Figure 2   NEC3 contract structure

Necessary clauses

Many standard form contracts presuppose that all projects follow a similar enough route under a particular procurement strategy for all the contract conditions to be the same, i.e. generic. Even in the context of a clear decision as to the procurement route and therefore the contract form, this is inflexible and tends to favour a 'form-filling' mentality, rather than a creative approach to assembling the appropriate contract for a particular project. There are parallels for this distinction in other areas of an architect's expertise; for example, when completing an NBS-style[17] specification, one approach would be to leave most standard clauses intact – just in case they prove useful, while the opposite approach would be to start from a blank sheet and to include only those clauses that are considered strictly necessary. NEC3 is analogous to the latter approach, which tends to result in shorter documentation, avoidance of extraneous or superfluous clauses and consequential clarity.

'Designing' the project-specific contract

While some organisations have deliberately put in place standard contract preparation procedures in order to maintain quality, it is clearly inadvisable to follow such procedures when assembling the contract conditions of an NEC contract. The whole point of the three-tier hierarchical structure is that it allows for the contract to be 'designed' as a tight fit for the needs of an individual project, and it is not only acceptable but positively to be expected that different main option and secondary option combinations will be chosen to augment the core clause sections for different projects. Even where projects are of a similar building type, or for the same client body, the decisions on appropriate options should be made afresh each time, in order to enable optimum performance of the NEC3 contract on any one project.

NEC3 is a proactive contract, requiring hands-on management from the outset, including putting it together. There is no default version of the contract and it simply will not be operable if its assembly does not follow the envisaged structure or is incomplete. NEC3 will appeal greatly in the context of wanting a pragmatic framework within which to manage real projects effectively. The skill set required of architects is such that they should be well equipped to respond to the need to assemble the contract creatively, carefully and in adequate consultation with their clients.

---

17. National Building Specification.

Core clauses

There are nine core clause sections, each of which deals with an individual concept (Figure 3).

Section 1
General

Section 2
The *Contractor's* main responsibilities

Section 3
Time

Section 4
Testing and Defects

Section 5
Payment

Section 6
Compensation events

Section 7
Title

Section 8
Risks and insurance

Section 9
Termination

Figure 3   NEC3 core clauses

The following provides an interpretive commentary on the salient points within those concepts, rather than simply paraphrasing all the clause content.

Core Clause Section 1: General

This general section is key to operating the entire contract and new users of NEC3 who have perhaps become used to skim-reading older forms of contract (whether because of familiarity or tedium!) would do well to be meticulous in working their way through this section. The drafting style throughout the contract is refreshingly succinct and the meaning and purpose of individual clauses should be relatively easy to discern. Ironically, there is more risk that the succinctness will be interpreted oversimplistically than that any clauses will be regarded as obtuse.

The first clause of the contract has sometimes been regarded as its most controversial:

> 10.1   The *Employer*, the *Contractor*, the *Project Manager* and the *Supervisor* shall act as stated in this contract and in a spirit of mutual trust and co-operation.

In the early years of NEC, this clause was probably regarded by many as aspirational, rather than legally binding; now, it is much more likely that a failure to act as required might be construed as a breach of contract. The statement in this clause has come to be regarded as virtually synonymous with the ethos of partnering. The progress of partnering has been such that it is no longer fanciful to ascribe legal obligation to that ethos (see *Partnering*, page 64). The ethos is also consistent with the concept of 'good faith' under civil law jurisdictions, which is a well-established legal obligation in most European countries.[18]

In view of the NEC provision for use in different jurisdictions, it is important to check the law of the contract, whether in terms of what is appropriate when filling out the Contract Data, or in terms of retrospectively assessing legal obligations (see *Jurisdiction*, page 71).

The explanation of identified[19] and defined[20] terms is extremely important to correct understanding and usage of all the following clauses and this part of the contract will become well thumbed by architects administering NEC3 contracts, whether acting as Project Manager, Supervisor, or both (see *People*, page 47).

NEC3 has an 'entire agreement' clause,[21] which has the usual purpose of improving clarity by excluding any prior agreements. The Contractor is not expected to do anything illegal or impossible.[22] There is also a 'prevention' clause,[23] which allocates the risk of unforeseeable events to the Employer.

Types of communication are specified under NEC3,[24] both in terms of type and timescale – this is a critical factor in improving project management (see *Communications*, page 56). It is acknowledged that ambiguities or inconsistencies could exist in the contract documents and provision is made to resolve any such items.[25]

---

18. E.g. 'Treu und Glauben' under German law.
19. In italics and identified in the Contract Data.
20. With Capital Initials and defined in core clause 11.2.
21. Core clause 12.4.
22. Core clause 18.
23. Core clause 19.
24. Core clause 13.
25. Core clause 17.

NEC3 envisages that the Contractor may need access to places that are not part of a building site as such and that there may also be reason to restrict access on a building site to specific areas – the combination of these being defined as the Working Areas.[26] This is a more sophisticated approach than simply giving a contractor 'possession' of a site and, in practice, allows better control and a manageable solution to any need to share spaces on a building site. There is provision for making additional areas available where this becomes necessary.[27]

NEC3 focuses throughout on efficient project management and contemporaneous resolution of any matters that could affect time, cost or quality (see *Dispute management*, page 56). The early warning provisions and the maintenance of a Risk Register are vital provisions in this respect.[28]

Core Clause Section 2: The Contractor's main responsibilities

In Providing the Works,[29] the Contractor is only bound by the content of the Works Information, which means in practice that the quality of the Works Information is of paramount importance in controlling the realisation of any building being constructed under NEC3 (see *Works Information*, page 45). Architects would typically be responsible for the production and co-ordination of the Works Information on building projects and will therefore be particularly interested in the relationship between its quality and that of the corresponding completed building.

The Contractor has potential responsibility for design of parts of a building, subject to individual project requirements.[30] In practice, those individual project requirements might suggest anywhere between 0% and 100% design by the Contractor, whether the percentage be of the entire building or of discrete constituent parts. The NEC3 *Black Book* enables architects to have tremendous freedom in deciding exactly the right split in terms of what design work is allocated to whom and at what stage of the project (see *Design*, page 54). The Contractor also has potential responsibility for design of Equipment;[31] i.e. typically on building projects, temporary works necessary to realise the permanent works. The Works Information is the correct place to accurately define any requirements for the Contractor to design any item, whether permanent or temporary. The Works Information is also the correct place to identify the parameters of the Employer's rights in relation to using any designs executed by the Contractor.[32]

The Contractor has responsibilities concerning provision of key staff and any necessary replacement of staff. The Contractor also has potential responsibility to co-operate with Others,[33] including sharing the Working Areas. In practice, these responsibilities are extremely useful project management aids, particularly as they recognise the multitude of external bodies and stakeholders who can be involved in today's building projects.

The Contractor has potentially onerous responsibilities concerning any subcontracting (see *Subcontracting*, page 63), although the correct discharge of those responsibilities reaps significant rewards in terms of efficiency and quality of outcome, which is arguably in both the Contractor's and the Employer's best interests.

---

26. Core clause 11.2 (18).
27. Core clause 15.
28. Core clause 16.
29. Core clause 11.2 (13).
30. Core clause 21.
31. Core clause 11.2 (7).
32. Core clause 22.
33. Core clause 11.2 (10).

In view of the potential international use of NEC3, the Contractor's responsibilities in relation to health and safety are not stated in the core clauses, but are to be stated in the Works Information specific to an individual project. Architects building in the UK need to be aware of this distinction and ensure that appropriate references to relevant legislation[34] are made in the project-specific Works Information.

Core Clause Section 3: Time

The temporal provisions of NEC3 are prescriptive, challenging and very good news. It is no exaggeration to state that architects have conventionally been in the hot seat in relation to delays on projects and that discharging their responsibilities with respect to extensions of time under many standard form contracts has become exceedingly difficult in the past decade. It is an area where responsible architects would be justified in suffering sleepless nights, given the potentially disastrous combination of 'responsibility without authority' which appears to exist in the drafting of some standard form contracts in relation to assessing responsibility for delay. The nub of the issue is that if an architect is expected to make such assessments objectively and in accordance with the critical temporal path of a project,[35] then doing so without the benefit of an appropriate programme from the contractor is well nigh impossible; producing such a programme independently might possibly be sensible if shown to the contractor, but is nevertheless illogical.

Where NEC3 differs radically from many other standard form contracts is in its approach to the provision by the Contractor of a programme, which can be seen to assist everyone involved in a project in achieving clarity and certainty of temporal outcome, both from the outset and as the project progresses.[36] The status of that programme, once initially accepted and subsequently reaccepted by the Project Manager,[37] is binding on both parties to an NEC3 building contract, i.e. Employer and Contractor alike.

NEC3 distinguishes between the *starting date* and the *first access date*, thus catering for the eventuality of early Contractor involvement prior to commencement of construction on-site.

The conventional distinction between a contractual completion date and the actual date of completion is made in NEC3 as well, the former being stated in the Contract Data and the latter being certified by the Project Manager.

NEC3 introduced the provision of Key Dates, which in practice can be very helpful on some relatively complex building projects where an Employer may need to ensure that critical dates along the way are controllable, without necessarily requiring Sectional Completion.[38]

A novel feature for architects to find in a standard form contract is the ability in NEC3 to instruct acceleration.[39] This provision should not be used lightly as it clearly has potential financial implications; however, there will be building clients and building projects where there would be undoubted benefit in the ability to invoke 'official' acceleration to achieve earlier completion of a project or part of a project.

Core clause Section 3 is one of the most fundamentally different concepts relative to other standard form building contracts; however, it is also one of the most rewarding sections of NEC3 for architects to get to grips with (see *Programme*, page 53).

---

34. The Construction (Design and Management) Regulations 2007.
35. *Henry Boot Construction (UK) Limited* v. *Malmaison Hotel 2000*.
36. Core clauses 31 & 32.
37. Core clause 11.2 (1).
38. Secondary option X5.
39. Core clause 36.

Core Clause Section 4: Testing and Defects

The role of the Supervisor will be new to architects using NEC3 for the first time (see *People*, page 47). The responsibilities in relation to quality are not merely advisory, as is often the case with a 'clerk of works' role; they are an integral part of the overall contract administration to be carried out on behalf of the Employer.

The multidisciplinary nature of NEC3 is such that foreseen testing and inspection of specific items is envisaged as a potential project requirement and this is provided for on the basis that it applies to any parts of a project so designated in the Works Information.[40] Historically, some building projects have not had any requirement for foreseen testing or inspection; however, there are now many contexts where this clear contractual provision will benefit projects (e.g. concrete cube testing for crushing strength, visual inspection of full scale mock-ups of façade materials, air-tightness testing for building regulations compliance etc.). It is important at design stage that architects give appropriate thought to necessary inspection of samples and testing requirements, in order that appropriate specification can be incorporated into the Works Information.

Core clause Section 4 also covers dealing with unforeseen testing and inspection, i.e. checking for defects. There are reciprocal obligations as between the Supervisor and the Contractor to notify each other of each Defect as soon as they find it (see *Defects*, page 55).

Core Clause Section 5: Payment

The operation in practice of the payment provisions within NEC3 will be heavily dependent on which main option is chosen. The primary reason for this is that both the definition of Defined Cost[41] and the definition of the Price for Work Done to Date[42] are different for each main option, as is to be expected in the context of each main option allowing a different payment mechanism. Architects initially observing projects under the NEC3 form of contract might find it helpful to look at the main option payment provisions simultaneously with the core clause payment provisions – this will be essential for any architect acting as Project Manager and therefore actually administering those payment provisions! It is also important to realise that the payment provisions under each of the main options rely on the proper execution of the relevant parts of the Contract Data in order to become fully operable. It is exceedingly rare under NEC3 for payment difficulties to arise if the contract has been assembled properly; however, if there has been any lack of rigour in doing so, it is fairly predictable that severe difficulties and unexpected outcomes can arise.

Architects should take particular note of the requirement to account for applicable tax, in addition to substantive sums, in amounts due for payment, as this is not usual in other standard form building contracts. Architects should also take note, where applicable, of the requirement to account for interest in the case of any corrections to substantive sums.

There is a deliberately draconian provision in the payment section which effectively withholds 25% of the amount due for payment until such time as a first programme is submitted by the Contractor. This is intended to severely disincentivise the Contractor from failing to fulfil the programme requirements in core clause Section 3 (Time)[43] because such failure would in turn make other provisions within the contract, notably the compensation event provisions, inoperable.[44]

---

40. Core clauses 40 & 41.
41. Main option clauses A11.2 (22), B11.2 (22), C11.2 (23), D11.2 (23), E11.2 (23) & F11.2 (24).
42. Main option clauses A11.2 (27), B11.2 (28), C11.2 (29), D11.2 (29), E11.2 (29) & F11.2 (29).
43. Core clause 31.1.
44. Core clause 63.3.

Core Clause Section 6: Compensation events

This section is regarded by many as the magnum opus of the NEC core clauses. Section 6 is certainly a section which received many comments in relation to the second edition of NEC and it is probably fair to say that it is the most amended section as between the second edition of NEC and the third edition, NEC3.

Essentially, the compensation event procedures in core clause Section 6 are intended to deal simultaneously with both the financial and the temporal consequences of foreseeable events which materialise during the course of the contract and which are at the Employer's risk.

The whole idea of 'compensation events' is pivotal to the successful operation of NEC3. In the context of risk management, it is important to acknowledge that all risks that materialise on a project are allocatable to one or other party to the contract for that project. The well-rehearsed, albeit somewhat glib, risk management advice that residual contractual risk should be allocated to the party best able to carry it is completely compatible with the concept of compensation events. The contractual list of compensation events,[45] while specific and exhaustive, is a powerful tool in appropriate risk allocation and risk management on an individual project. Anyone questioning how a prescriptive, generic list of compensation events can be flexible enough to manage a plethora of varying risk profiles on different projects would be missing a key feature of NEC3: the author of the Works Information is in virtually complete control of the project's destiny! Notifying, assessing and implementing compensation events all take place relative to that project-specific Works Information and Accepted Programme, and outcomes will therefore be as varied as the risk profiles and the Works Information and Accepted Programme content for individual projects.

By inextricably linking time with money and by relating both to objective contract documents, i.e. the Works Information and the Accepted Programme, it is possible through correct operation of core clause Section 6 to maintain throughout any project contract both a running final account and a predicted date for completion, both of which will normally[46] be a maximum of three weeks behind real time (see *Change control*, page 57).

Core Clause Section 7: Title

On most projects, core clause Section 7 probably attracts the least attention of all the core clause sections; certainly its content and brevity indicate that architects can distil the salient points relatively quickly.

The concept of Working Areas is helpful to architects in giving clarity over ownership of, and right to payment for, materials intended to be included in the works[47] but which are not yet on the actual building site. Conversely, there should be no question of the Contractor expecting payment for any materials stored outside the Working Areas, unless the NEC3 contract has been executed to include advanced payment.[48]

This section also ensures that the Employer is not left with unwanted temporary items at the end of the project[49] and that there is clarity over items found within the site during construction.[50]

---

45. Core clause 60.1.
46. Core clause 62.3.
47. As identified in Contract Data Part One.
48. Secondary option X14.
49. Core clause 72.
50. Core clause 73.

Core Clause Section 8: Risks and insurance

The respective generic risk allocation as between the Employer and the Contractor is set out in this section.[51] This should be distinguished from the project-specific risk allocation, which is largely defined by the content of the Works Information.

The default is that generic risks are required to be covered by insurance and that insurance is taken out by the Contractor in joint names, unless the Contract Data specifically gives any insurance obligations to the Employer. There is an insurance table[52] summarising the type of cover required, which divides risks into four categories: (1) works insurance, (2) Equipment (temporary works/machinery) insurance, (3) public liability (persons and property) insurance and (4) employer liability insurance. The Contract Data is the correct place to identify any switch of insurance obligations from Contractor to Employer, as well as any additional insurance requirements, e.g. professional indemnity insurance.

Given the potential for NEC3 to be used in different countries and jurisdictions, there is a need to ensure that both the types and levels of insurance cover are in accordance with the applicable national law and that the Contract Data is filled out accordingly.

There is a reciprocal requirement for whichever party is responsible for taking out the insurances to submit proof of insurance (certificates and/or policies) to the other party for acceptance (see *Communications*, page 56). There is also a reciprocal right for a party to counter-charge the other party for having to take out insurance in the absence of proof from that other party, if they are responsible for taking out such insurance, that the required policy is in place.[53]

Core Clause Section 9: Termination

This is perhaps the least easy core clause section to digest, in that it sets out specific rules to be followed in the event of termination by either the Contractor or the Employer. These rules are relatively complex and the only consolation is that this entire core clause section will be relatively rarely used. One of the main changes to this core clause section as between the second edition of NEC and NEC3 is the omission of 'Disputes' in the current version, i.e. 'Termination and Disputes' has become 'Termination' only (see *Dispute resolution options*, page 41).

The Contractor has a right to terminate, but only for reasons set out in the Termination Table,[54] whereas the Employer may terminate for any reason, albeit the procedures and the amounts due on termination reflect the justification of a reason.

---

51. Core clauses 80 & 81.
52. Core clause 84.
53. Core clauses 86 & 87.
54. Core clause 90.2.

Main option clauses

There are six main options (Figure 4), a single one of which must be chosen in order to provide a payment mechanism and make an NEC3 contract operable.

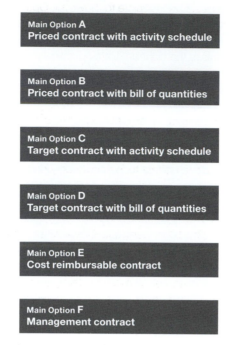

Main Option A
Priced contract with activity schedule

Main Option B
Priced contract with bill of quantities

Main Option C
Target contract with activity schedule

Main Option D
Target contract with bill of quantities

Main Option E
Cost reimbursable contract

Main Option F
Management contract

Figure 4   NEC3 main option clauses

It has sometimes been questioned whether NEC contracts are fairer – i.e. have a better balanced allocation of risk – than other standard form contracts? The only correct answer to such a question is 'it depends'. One of the key things it depends upon is a rational choice of the contractual payment mechanism, i.e. the one – and one only – main option. Risk allocation can be significantly altered on any project by virtue of the choice of main option. New users of NEC3 should not treat the main options as a pick and mix where they necessarily have to try all the flavours! It is entirely to be expected that professionals and their clients who work predominantly in one sector of the construction industry will not go through the whole array of NEC3 main options. Architects working on building projects will possibly specialise in a certain building type with a specific client base and so might well choose to use the same main option on numerous projects. This is most certainly not because NEC3 contracts should be 'standardised' in a practice, but because it is foreseeable that when proper procurement analysis takes place on a number of similar projects, the same NEC3 main option may consistently provide the best contractual fit for each particular project.

In summary, the choice of main option is crucial to the successful operation of an NEC3 contract. Architects should keep an open mind in analysing the right choice for any one project, but they should not be tempted to choose a different main option 'just for a change'!

Main Option A: Priced contract with activity schedule

Option A essentially creates a lump sum contract, suitable for a range of building projects. Most architects who are experienced in administering other standard form contracts on a traditional procurement route will probably find this main option the easiest one to relate to; however, Option A is not restricted to traditional procurement. Architects should not be concerned if they regularly decide, after carrying out a full analysis of procurement strategy for each building project, that Option A is the most appropriate NEC3 main option to put forward to their client.

The payment mechanism under Option A is incredibly straightforward, in that the Contractor is entitled to be paid for each completed activity. It is important to realise the significance of activities having to be completed. First, 'completed' does not mean nearly finished, it means 100% finished; the Contractor is thus incentivised to stay on programme. Second, there is no need for either debate or specific valuation expertise in order to determine the value of a completed activity; it will simply be the monetary value ascribed to the relevant activity within the Contractor's Activity Schedule. This is the reason why quantity surveyors need not perform a conventional valuation role in relation to NEC3 Option A contracts.

Those who remain unfamiliar with activity schedules under any standard form building contract sometimes question why an NEC3 activity has to be 100% complete. The answer to this is simply that there is no mechanism for assessing the value of partially completed activities. While it might be very easy and relatively accurate to prorate, for example, five courses of a 10m length of blockwork which is to be 15 courses high and the same length when complete, it would clearly be much more difficult to prorate, for example, a partially completed mechanical or electrical services installation. The benefits of allowing the Contractor to split up a project into activities relating to appropriate work elements, in relation to both logical progress on site and cash flow, would be completely lost if the Employer still had to ensure that some sort of pricing document be produced in tandem, solely to enable partially completed work elements to be valued. Indeed, there would be significant scope for disputes to arise due to potentially conflicting methods for assessment of value.

If difficulties do arise with NEC3 Option A contracts, it is likely to be due to a lack of understanding of the principles of activity schedules per se, rather than necessarily the requirements of NEC3. It is perhaps significant that while a number of standard form contracts have offered activity schedules as an alternative payment mechanism for some time, there is relatively little anecdotal evidence of their use in the building sector of the construction industry, and perhaps even less evidence of their success where occasionally used under other standard form building contracts.

It may be helpful to consider some particular criteria that contractors should give due regard to when splitting up a project to prepare an activity schedule:

- Does the activity schedule cover the entire works? That is, does there need to be a catch-all activity for 'everything else' other than the listed activities, or can the list of activities be exhaustive? 'Missing' activities could clearly lead to difficulties over entitlement to payment.

- Upon what basis does a particular project lend itself to be split up? For example, trade-related elements, demarcated geographical areas on the site etc. In practice this will depend on the size and nature of the particular project; many projects may well benefit from being split up on a two- or three-tier basis. There is no magic 'right number' of activities on any project; too few activities could lead to cash flow difficulties, but too many activities could become an administrative burden. It may be advantageous to management clarity to group activities that are interdependent.

- What is the relationship between physical activities and management activities? Are there benefits in separating them, or are they inextricably linked?

- Items that are conventionally priced under the heading of 'Preliminaries' are still activities and should appear in an activity schedule accordingly. This is essential under the NEC3 form of contract because of the NEC principle of inextricably linking time with money.

- Are the individual physical activities logically related to technical requirements in executing the works on-site? For example, if a concrete pour has to be done in two stages because of temporary works obstructions then it should clearly also comprise two separate activities!

- Have the durations of activities been considered in relation to contractual payment intervals? For example, if all the substructure concrete is to be poured sequentially, but that sequence will last for five weeks and the payment interval is four weeks, then it will assist cash flow if that physical sequence is split into two activities.

A question that is commonly asked is how would the Option A provisions work in the case of a Contractor realising either that an activity cannot be completed as a discrete element of work or that it would be better to change the methodology for an activity? It is also often asked how the Option A provisions should work in the case of a change to the required work under the contract affecting one or more activities. The key to answering these points is to understand the relationship between the Activity Schedule and the Accepted Programme.

In the case of the Contractor wishing to change the sequence of work on-site, the Contractor is entitled to do so but must alter and resubmit the Activity Schedule, if necessary with a correspondingly revised programme.[55]

In the case of an instruction to change the works required under the contract, the Contractor is obliged to change the Activity Schedule accordingly.[56]

For routine payments as a project progresses, Option A simply requires the Project Manager, possibly with assistance, to be capable of assessing whether any activity is 100% complete and should therefore be included in the certified sum for payment. In practice, any architect who has been involved in the preparation and co-ordination of the design documentation in the Works Information and who has studied the Contractor's Activity Schedule should have no difficulty in deciding when an activity is 100% complete.

In addition to routine payments, the Option A payment mechanism also has to deal with any payments that become due as a result of instructed changes under the contract. Option A provides for a Fee to be applied in the case of compensation events, that Fee being made up of two percentages, which may be different: one to be applied to the Defined Cost of subcontracted work and one to be applied to the Defined Cost of other work.[57]

---

55. Main option A clause 54.2.
56. Main option A clause 63.12.
57. Core clause 11.2 (8).

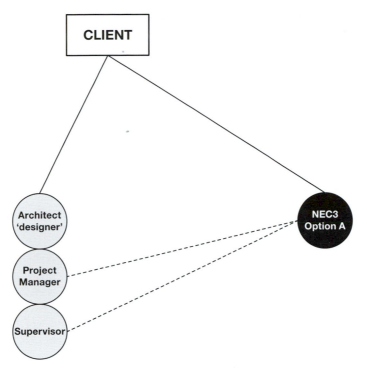

Figure 5   Main Option A: architect acts as Project Manager and Supervisor

Main Option B: Priced contract with bill of quantities

Option B effectively creates a remeasurement contract, because the inaccuracy margin permissible in the Bill of Quantities without it becoming grounds for a compensation event is minimal. If architects are putting Option B forward to their clients as the most appropriate payment mechanism for a particular project, they should emphasise that it does not create a lump sum contract and that the potential risk for quantity changes would rest with the Employer.[58]

This main option is possibly the one that many architects who are experienced in administering other standard form contracts on a traditional procurement route will tend to gravitate towards, if only because of the familiarity of the term 'Priced contract with bill of quantities'. In practice, this could cause difficulties for architects and their clients alike unless there is complete clarity over the issue of remeasurement, i.e. complete understanding and acceptance of the fact that because Option B does not automatically create a lump sum contract, the price would not necessarily remain fixed, even if no changes were instructed.

This is not a defect in NEC3, but rather a natural consequence of the NEC principle of flexibility and its design as a contract that can cater for a potentially vast range of project requirements. Any architects who have worked on multidisciplinary projects, such as rail infrastructure, are likely to have come across the custom of remeasuring engineering quantities. Equally, architects who have worked on refurbishment projects are likely to be familiar with standard form building contracts that are either 'without quantities' or 'with approximate quantities', i.e. contracts that assume measurement or remeasurement of quantities.

---

58. Main option B clause 60.4.

Option B envisages the conventional preparation of a Bill of Quantities on behalf of the Employer at tender stage and it foresees the possibility that individual lump sums may be allocated to specific items included in the scope of work to be carried out by the Contractor. Option B provides a payment mechanism where the Contractor is entitled to be paid for each item in the Bill of Quantities on the basis of quantity multiplied by the rate and is entitled to be paid for lump sums. This accounts for why employers will normally retain quantity surveyors or cost consultants in relation to NEC3 Option B contracts, both for preparation of the Bill of Quantities pre-contract and to perform a valuation role post-contract.

One of the critical differences between Option A and Option B in the context of building projects is that the fees for preparation of the Option B Bill of Quantities will be borne directly by the Employer, whereas the Option A Activity Schedule will be funded by tendering contractors as part of their 'bidding risk'. Furthermore, while Option A tender periods should reflect the Activity Schedule production time, this is unlikely to increase the length of a pre-contract programme by as much as allowing adequate time for the production of the Bill of Quantities under Option B.

One slight 'philosophical' anomaly between Option B and Option A is in the context of any individually allocated lump sums under Option B relative to activities under Option A. The Option B payment mechanism allows for proportional payment for lump sums on the basis of proportional completion of each lump sum. This is in direct contrast to the Option A payment mechanism of avoiding proportional payment and only allowing payment of 100% complete activities. Option B does not, therefore, assist in incentivising the Contractor to stay on programme in the way that Option A does. It is also foreseeable that a dispute could potentially arise under Option B as to the precise proportion of a lump sum that had been completed at the end of a particular payment interval. While it is consistent with the principle of a Bill of Quantities that proportional payment takes place, it is tempting to conclude that Option B is much less radical than Option A in its approach to incentivisation and dispute avoidance. To use the 'carrot and stick' analogy, Option A seems to proffer plenty of carrots, whereas Option B seems to still rely more on sticks.

Perhaps the moral if using Option B is to limit lump sums to items that can easily be proportioned and ensure that the accuracy of quantities is meticulous. However, in the context of all but the most simple of building projects, the ubiquitous 'M&E' installation is likely to present a challenge in relation to both of those aims.

In addition to routine payments under Option B, the payment mechanism also has to deal with payments that may become due as a result of instructed changes under the contract.[59] As with Option A, Option B provides for a Fee to be applied in the case of compensation events, that Fee being made up of two percentages, which may be different: one to be applied to the Defined Cost of subcontracted work and one to be applied to the Defined Cost of other work.

---

59. Main option B clause 63.13.

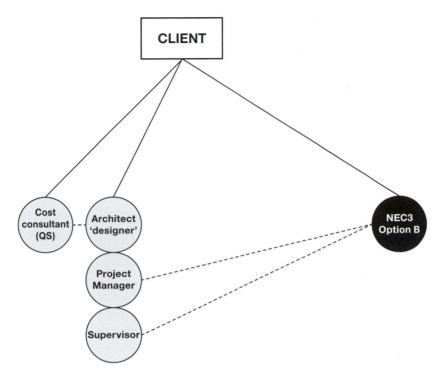

Figure 6   Main Option B: architect acts as Project Manager and Supervisor

Main Option C: Target contract with activity schedule

A target cost is agreed at the outset, with an incentive to the Contractor to achieve or to better the target in the form of a share in any savings. The cost of the project is distributed into an Activity Schedule prepared by the Contractor, in a manner similar to Option A. The Activity Schedule under Option C is perhaps best understood as a distribution of the costs making up the Target Cost, where the sum of the constituent parts (activities) may or may not be greater than the whole Target Cost, depending on what the Contractor actually spends in terms of Defined Cost (see *Defined Cost*, page 44). Conversely, the sum of the constituent parts (activities) under an Option A Activity Schedule equals the whole contract lump sum. This distinction has an important impact on risk profile and incentivisation. It is one of many examples in NEC3 of where the status and implementation of things (whether documents such as an Activity Schedule or defined terms such as Price for Work Done to Date) are deliberately somewhat different depending on which main option has been chosen.

Target incentivisation

Note that with an NEC3 Option C contract, the allocation of risk can be significantly weighted by the share percentages allocated to each party to the contract – hence the expression 'pain/gain' share. The intention is that the proportions are agreed, rather than imposed, as much of the potential benefit will be lost if excessive risk is priced as a contingency item, which may or may not materialise. It would not be unusual for the share percentages for any pain and any gain to be unequal, subject to a proper assessment of which party is best able to carry certain project risks.

While target cost procurement strategies are not unique to NEC3, an architect's first encounter with target costs may well have been, or is likely to be, via the NEC. There are now a number of examples of repeat clients using NEC3 Option C contracts, both in order to better performance relative to other procurement strategies and in order to compare performance between their own projects and supply chain teams.[60]

In implementing a target cost strategy, the first long-standing concept to relegate is that of having a contract sum – there isn't one! There is only the 'Target Cost' calculated for that individual project. An obvious, but sadly sometimes overlooked, factor in the success of target cost contracts is the accuracy of the cost plan upon which the target cost is based. Typically, most employers contemplating a target cost procurement strategy will be experienced clients, building projects of relatively large size, above average complexity and with sensitive accountability for spending. Such clients often have experienced in-house procurement advisors or might seek sophisticated procurement advice from consultants, which has both advantages and disadvantages. If the calibre of the advice given is high, there will undoubtedly be an emphasis on detailed risk analysis and risk management, which in turn is likely to lead to a very careful setting of both the Target Cost and the pain/gain share percentages.

However, experience from over 20 years' use of NEC contracts suggests that very occasionally a somewhat 'unreconstructed' approach to risk management is adopted, whereby an employer is encouraged to shunt as much risk onto a contractor as possible. This way of thinking may have had its origins in older, more adversarial standard form contracts and may still be considered appropriate in some circumstances. However, if it were to lead to an employer managing to sign up a contractor on an NEC3 Option C contract with an artificially low Target Cost and a share percentage of 100% in any overspend relative to that target, it does not take much imagination to realise that the outcome might be very painful indeed – and not just for the Contractor, but also for the Employer.

The key point is that starting on the basis of the right Target Cost is even more important than agreeing the right share percentages for the risk of deviation from that cost. One of the most obvious ways of improving the accuracy of the Target Cost is to involve the contractor(s) bidding for the work as they ought to have access to at least as accurate figures as cost consultants. If the list of contractors bidding for a job has been drawn up appropriately, such contractors ought to be in a strong position not only to contribute to accurate cost forecasting, but also to critique design solutions and offer useful value engineering input. This is not an NEC-specific point; however, an NEC3 Option C contract will have a massively improved chance of success if there really is 'a spirit of mutual trust and co-operation' between Employer and Contractor teams with regard to the design of the contract as well as the building.

---

60. E.g. healthcare and food retail sector clients.

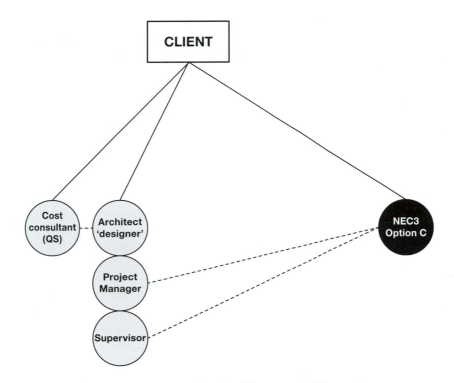

Figure 7   Main Option C: architect acts as Project Manager and Supervisor

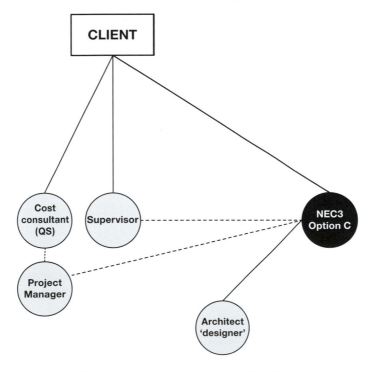

Figure 8   Main Option C: architect employed by design and build contractor

Main Option D: Target contract with bill of quantities

As with Option C, the incentive to achieve the target relies on the requirement that any overspend is shared in pre-agreed proportions between the parties.

With Option D, as with Option C, the fairness of the so-called 'pain/gain share' relies both on the cost planning being sufficiently accurate to arrive at a realistic Target Cost and on the share percentages and share ranges agreed to form part of the contract.

With Option D, as with Option B, the minimal inaccuracy margin permissible in the Bill of Quantities without it becoming grounds for a compensation event effectively creates a remeasurement contract.

Looking at the particular payment mechanism provided in Option D in relation to building projects, there is clearly a need to assess risks in three areas: the accuracy of the Bill of Quantities, the accuracy of the cost plan upon which the Target Cost is based and the pain/gain share percentages. The overall risk profile that may emerge on a project under Option D could perhaps be a step too far for many architects and their building clients, as it would require spending a disproportionate amount of time on pre-contract analysis and therefore a disproportionate amount of money on cost consultancy fees. This is not so much a criticism of the payment mechanism represented by Option D, but rather a recognition of the vast number of project types and sizes which NEC3 is intended to cater for. Not all of the main option payment mechanisms will be equally suited to all project types or sizes.

The following is an example of a risk profile for a building project that might benefit from using Option D to create high levels of motivation for both Employer and Contractor to achieve a well-managed outcome:

- a large commercial project that includes infrastructure elements

- an experienced client wishing to keep control of the pricing document, i.e. the Bill of Quantities

- a potential for early contractor involvement, which could lead to a negotiated Target Cost

- an acceptance that quantities of many items would be remeasured

- a desire for incremental pain/gain share percentages, i.e. where any spending over or under the target cost is not penalised or rewarded absolutely, but in proportion to the extent of deviation from the Target Cost, upwards or downwards

- a desire for reciprocal pain/gain share percentages, i.e. not necessarily entirely equal share percentages for the Employer and the Contractor as between 'painful overspend' and 'gainful underspend', but a correlation between the share percentage allocated to a party and that party's ability to manage the risk.

There is anecdotal evidence among NEC3 users that Option D has been significantly less used on building projects than Option C, where an incentivised Target Cost is desirable. This is perhaps encouraging, as it indicates that NEC3 users are becoming quite discerning about risk management on building projects.

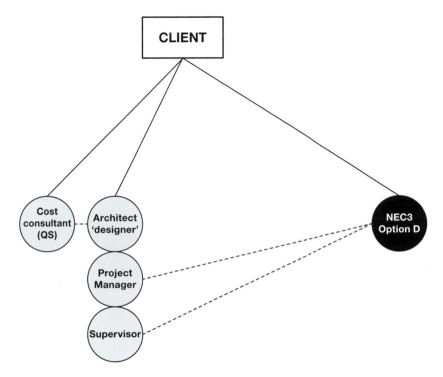

Figure 9   Main Option D: architect acts as Project Manager and Supervisor

Main Option E: Cost reimbursable contract

An 'open book' accounting policy is intended to operate, with the Contractor being paid at Defined Cost[61] plus a percentage Fee for profit and overheads.

Open book accounting is a concept that has been completely embraced in some quarters of the construction industry and yet is still regarded with a degree of disbelief in others. The idea of disclosing actual invoices and declaring profit and overhead percentages also seems to find more favour in some countries than others. Ultimately, comfort with a payment mechanism that is based on open book accounting is as much a matter of culture as it is of contractual arrangements.

Option E is predicated on the Contractor being able to recover costs and overheads and make a profit, but there will be some building clients whose reaction to this approach might be 'why should contractors carry no risk?'. Experience should tell the building industry that simply shunting risks in the opposite direction rarely benefits clients, as contractors who are expected to gamble in terms of their ability to make any profit will try to protect their interests. This is not an NEC3 phenomenon, but merely human nature playing its part. With any building contract, unless there is a payment mechanism that acknowledges profit as a right for contractors, all contractors will tend to attempt to build in contingencies of some sort as a way of protecting their legitimate expectations in carrying out work for clients.

---

61. Main option E clause 11.2 (23).

As envisaged with any cost reimbursable type contract, Option E permits an early start on-site, with relatively little final information available to the Contractor. While this represents a risk to the Employer in terms of outturn cost on a building project, the decision to use any of the NEC3 main options should be founded on sound procurement analysis (as discussed in Chapter 1, *Procurement strategy*): it may well be that the Employer has set time as a key parameter on a particular project, in which case Option E may well offer advantages.

The manner in which an element of building work is costed under Option E is independent of the timing of the instruction to carry out that element of work. That is because of the way in which payment at intervals is assessed under Option E, it makes no difference to the calculations whether the assessment includes items that were part of the contract at the outset, additional items that have been instructed post-contract, or a mixture of the two. However, because of the inextricable link under NEC3 between time and money within the compensation event procedure, the contract programme will clearly be extended by significant post-contract instructions. Architects will need to weigh up carefully in their procurement analysis with their clients how best to control not only the parameter of time relative to the other parameters, but also the potential benefits of an early start on-site – which Option E is suited to – relative to a longer duration on-site, which could arise from compensation events.

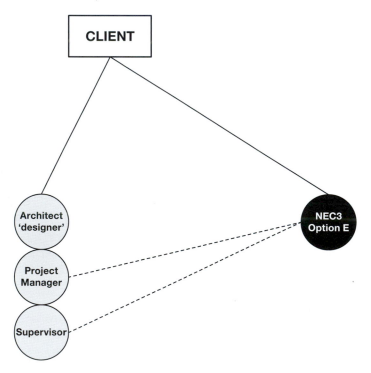

Figure 10   Main Option E: architect acts as project manager and supervisor

Main Option F: Management contract

There is anecdotal evidence that this main option has been the least used of all the NEC3 main options, across all sectors of the construction industry. Perhaps the reason for this is simply that the other five main options already offer significant flexibility of payment mechanisms and that NEC3 as a whole offers significant tailoring of procurement routes; i.e. a management style procurement route can be achieved under NEC3 without necessarily incorporating Option F.

The intention with Option F is that the Contractor manages the subcontract packages and prepares forecasts of the total Defined Cost[62] of all work and receives this plus a percentage Fee.

Possibly the best way for architects to assess the relative benefits of Option F when advising their clients on the assembly of an NEC3 contract is to focus on the degree of subcontracting desired and on how well prepared the scope of those subcontract packages is likely to be at the point when the NEC3 contract is to be entered into.

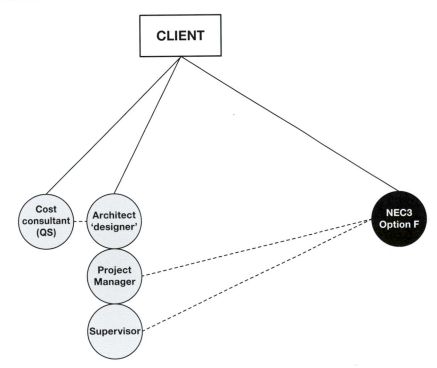

Figure 11   Main Option F: architect acts as Project Manager and Supervisor

---

62. Main option F clause 11.2 (24).

Secondary option clauses

The secondary options (Figure 12) can be operated on a pick and mix basis, in any combination, in order to tailor the contract as closely as possible to the needs of any particular project.

Secondary Option X1
Price adjustment for inflation

Secondary Option X2
Changes in the law

Secondary Option X3
Multiple currencies

Secondary Option X4
Parent company guarantee

Secondary Option X5
Sectional Completion

Secondary Option X6
Bonus for early Completion

Secondary Option X7
Delay damages

Note:
Options X8–X11 are not used in the *Black Book*

Secondary Option X12
Partnering

Secondary Option X13
Performance bond

Secondary Option X14
Advanced payment to the *Contractor*

Secondary Option X15
Limitation of the *Contractor's* liability for his design to reasonable skill and care

Secondary Option X16
Retention

Secondary Option X17
Low performance damages

Secondary Option X18
Limitation of liability

Note:
Option X19 is not used in the *Black Book*

Secondary Option X20
Key Performance Indicators

Secondary Option Y(UK)2
The Housing Grants, Construction and Regeneration Act 1996

Note:
Jurisdiction specific

Secondary Option Y(UK)3
The Contracts (Rights of Third Parties) Act 1999

Secondary Option Z
Additional conditions of contract

Figure 12   NEC3 secondary option clauses

These secondary options broadly fall into two categories:

- **Options which introduce choice in standard procedures**
  These secondary options contain processes that conventionally have been included in the contract conditions of standard form contracts whether needed or not, i.e. without giving a choice. An example of such a process would be Secondary Option X16: Retention.

- **Options which introduce additional standard procedures**
  These secondary options contain processes that conventionally have not been available in standard form contract conditions without the introduction of bespoke drafting. An example of such a process would be Secondary Option X3: Multiple currencies.

It is important to note that there is no obligation to introduce any of the secondary options; an NEC3 contract is operable with none of them included. Conversely, most of the secondary options are not mutually exclusive to one another, i.e. in theory, most of the secondary options could be included together in an NEC3 contract, the exception being that Secondary Option X20: Key Performance Indicators is not used with Secondary Option X12: Partnering. However, some of the secondary options and individual main options are mutually exclusive; this is not for the sake of complexity, but rather a direct response to the practicalities of project management. The logic behind the prohibition of any incompatible options becomes clear in looking at the individual secondary options.

Secondary Option X1: Price adjustment for inflation

[Used only with main options A, B, C or D]

Architects and their building clients will be familiar with standard form contracts offering the potential for the Employer to carry the risk of price increases. However, building clients in the UK have for decades been reluctant to take on this risk voluntarily and it is fairly unlikely that Secondary Option X1 would be put forward on a building project in the UK. The provision is offered to cater for sectors where it is more usual for the Employer to be well placed to carry the risk of price increases. It is also offered in recognition of NEC3 potentially being used in countries with high inflation, where the Contractor may be unwilling or unable to carry such a risk without being priced out of contention.

The reason that Secondary Option X1 is only used with main options A, B, C or D is simply that the payment mechanisms under main options E and F already entitle the Contractor to be paid on the basis of costs which include any inflation at the time of payment.

Secondary Option X2: Changes in the law

The risk of legislative changes during the currency of a contract is clearly higher under some jurisdictions than others. There is also the issue of whether a change in the law in a particular country is applied retrospectively or not. The impact on construction contracts will consequently be quite variable, depending on where the project is. Looking specifically at building contracts in the UK, the perceived risk is very low, although the procurement route will have an influence. For example, the risk of changes in the Building Regulations per se is quite high; however, because such changes do not apply retrospectively and adequate notice is given of their coming into force, the actual risk on a particular project is normally quite low. The procurement route will have an impact on the risk, as it may make a difference as to which party to the building contract would be liable for post-contract legislative changes. Using the same example of Building Regulations, the Contractor might be at greater risk under a design and build procurement route, where there is a long time period between entering into the contract and sign-off of any design packages requiring Building Regulations approval.

Architects and their building clients will need to consider the merits of this secondary option with regard to a particular project. Typically, it is not an option that would be considered necessary on many building projects in the UK. Where the Contractor is to be responsible for large amounts of design or is working on a project of long duration, there might be a financial advantage to the Employer at tender stage in incorporating this secondary option and accepting a risk that would otherwise rest with the Contractor.

In the case of working on projects in other countries, architects would need to be familiar with the differences in default risk in those countries. For example, in Germany the risk of changes in the law pertaining to technological standards as the project progresses, i.e. not retrospectively, would as a default rest with the Contractor.[63]

Secondary Option X3: Multiple currencies

[Used only with main options A or B]

It is increasingly common on construction projects for components to be imported from other countries. NEC3 is designed potentially to be used in any country, so whether, for example, Japanese air-handling units and German curtain walling are being imported for a UK building project, or Swiss precast concrete elements are being exported for a Chinese hydroelectric project, there are many situations where contractors may have to pay for components in more than one currency.

The idea behind Secondary Option X3 is that the Employer might be in a better position to carry the risk of currency fluctuations than the Contractor. In such a case, by incorporating Secondary Option X3, the Employer can agree to pay for certain items in their currency of origin (e.g. yen or euros), while other items are paid for in the default currency of the contract[64] (e.g. pounds sterling). The use of Secondary Option X3 therefore allows the exchange rate risk to be managed by the Employer rather than the Contractor.

The amount of payment in other currencies is capped in the contract to an agreed level and an exchange rate is stated. In practice, this means that where Secondary Option X3 is used, the Employer has the ability to manage the exchange rate risk in quite a sophisticated manner, such as by the use of hedging finance with forward contracts etc. Such a facility is particularly critical in times of exchange rate volatility, such as the 2008 to 2011 period.

Clients and their architects might feel that Secondary Option X3 requires excessive financial management skills; however, it should be seen as the option that it is, and it is clearly more suited to some clients than others. It should also be taken into consideration that some contractors are perfectly able to manage exchange rate risk without detriment to employers – an obvious example of this would be a multinational contracting firm with offices in both countries and therefore constantly using both currencies.

Any decision to use Secondary Option X3 will be entirely dependent on the specific project and client organisation.

63. anerkannte Regeln der Technik [recognised rules of technology (state of the art)].
64. Stated in Contract Data Part One.

Secondary Option X4: Parent company guarantee

The concept of Secondary Option X4 will be familiar to architects who are used to working on larger projects. Experienced clients who procure high-value projects often require some form of security for the performance of contractors. A parent company guarantee may be an appropriate form of security, albeit it relies on a particular contractor having a parent company.

This might be a useful provision on large-scale building projects and is relatively easy to implement by virtue of it being a 'standard' optional clause.

Where Secondary Option X4 is being considered for a building contract, it should ideally be done in the context of considering as an alternative Secondary Option X13: Performance bond. While the two secondary options are not mutually exclusive, it might be considered somewhat excessive to include both; it might also be unnecessarily expensive, given that both forms of security will normally attract a fee or premium payment.

Secondary Option X5: Sectional Completion

This will be a very familiar concept to most architects. As in other standard form contracts, this provision allows for different parts of a project to be completed sequentially. It is intended for use where a client requirement for such sequential completion is foreseeable from the outset.

Secondary Option X5 can be implemented on the basis that the entire project is split into particular sections, or on the basis that critical parts are identified as discrete sections, with the remainder being left within the 'whole of the works'. When using Secondary Option X5, care should be taken to ensure that there is complete clarity as to which parts of the works fall into a particular section; depending on the nature of work to be done, this may require detailed written and/or graphic descriptions to be included within the Works Information.

The Contract Data needs to be filled out with particular care when Secondary Option X5 is used. If the project has been split up into sections, then it follows that in the Contract Data the *completion date* for the whole of the works will be the same date as the *completion date* for the last identified section. If only certain critical parts have been identified as discrete sections, then the *completion date* for the whole of the works will be a later date than the *completion date* for the latest identified section.

In using Secondary Option X5, it follows that while not all of the works need be allocated to one of the sections, if a project team feels more comfortable doing so then the last identified section would effectively be 'and everything else', and the Completion Date for the whole of the works would be the same date as the completion date for that last identified section.

Secondary Option X6: Bonus for early Completion

This is likely to be an unfamiliar concept to most project teams in the building sector. It is perhaps helpful to see the idea of employers rewarding contractors for finishing early as no more than the converse of employers penalising contractors for finishing late. That is not to say that there is any necessary connection between the two under any form of building contract, but rather a way of comprehending the partnering principles behind Secondary Option X6, i.e. incentivisation and reciprocity of potential benefits.

In completing the Contract Data for Secondary Option X6, note will need to be taken of whether Secondary Option X6 is to operate on a single *completion date*, or on sectional completion dates because Secondary Option X5 is also included.

Secondary Option X7: Delay damages

This will be a very familiar concept to most project teams in the building sector. As in other standard form contracts, this provision allows employers to legitimately penalise contractors under the contract for finishing late. In implementing Secondary Option X7 under English law, it is important to remember that actual penalties are unenforceable and that the delay damages entered into the Contract Data must remain a genuine pre-estimate of the Employer's loss if the Contractor were to finish late.

Architects using NEC3 for the first time may be somewhat surprised to find that delay damages are optional, as similar damages are a well-established norm under other standard form contracts.[65] However, experienced NEC users are likely to look at the range of contractual measures available to incentivise contractors to stay on programme; it would be a waste of NEC3's potential to use Secondary Option X7 only because of its familiarity. In isolation, a negative incentive is a somewhat blunt instrument with which to tackle the issue of keeping complex building projects on programme. Hence, there is an argument for at least considering the relationship between Secondary Options X7 and X6.

There is also a need to look at an NEC3 contract holistically, as the perceived need to include Secondary Option X7 would almost certainly be judged differently on a building project under an Option A contract than under an Option E contract.

As with Secondary Option X6, in completing the Contract Data for Secondary Option X7, note will need to be taken of whether Secondary Option X7 is to operate on a single *completion date*, or on sectional completion dates because Secondary Option X5 is also included.

Secondary Option X12: Partnering

Secondary Option X12 is a subject in its own right and is discussed in more detail in Chapter 4 in the context of collaborative working as a whole – see *Partnering*, page 64.

The key message in relation to Secondary Option X12 is that it acts as extra cement with which to ensure the partnering relationship stays together and that it can achieve sophisticated aims. Secondary Option X12 is not the sole vehicle for creating a partnering relationship in the first instance: that is NEC3 itself.

Secondary Option X13: Performance bond

As with Secondary Option X4, the provision for providing a form of security to employers for the performance of contractors will be a familiar concept to architects who are used to working on larger projects. In this case, the security is ultimately provided by a bank or insurer, not the contracting organisation.

While this provision is in principle relatively easy to implement, by virtue of it being a 'standard' optional clause, care must be taken over stating the amount of the performance bond required,[66] describing the form of the bond required[67] and outlining the type of surety[68] that will be acceptable.

---

65. Liquidated and ascertained damages.
66. To be stated in Contract Data Part One.
67. To be stated in the Works Information.
68. The Project Manager has to accept the bank or insurer providing the Option X13 performance bond.

Where Secondary Option X13 is being considered for a building contract, it would normally not be sensible to include both Secondary Option X13 and Secondary Option X4 (parent company guarantee) as this would be somewhat excessive. This is not an NEC3-specific point, but rather common sense in the context of how best to protect employers against potential non-performance of contractors.

Secondary Option X14: Advanced payment to the Contractor

This provision for the Employer to make an advanced payment to the Contractor is something which will rarely be considered on some types of building project, but will be regarded as almost essential on others. As with many of the secondary options, this is not a novel concept; NEC3 is merely recognising common contractual requirements and pre-drafting provisions for such requirements in order that they may be picked off the contractual 'shelf' and suitably mixed with the other contract clauses to achieve the required overall 'recipe'.

An example of when this secondary option would be beneficial on a building project is where a large amount of prefabricated structural steelwork is part of the scope of the project and its lead-in time is critical but the fabricator requires the raw steel to be purchased in advance of the fabrication.

Secondary Option X14 can operate in two ways. First, the Employer can simply agree to pay a sum of money in advance to the Contractor for a particular expenditure and this sum is then paid back in instalments[69] at payment assessment intervals. Second, where large sums of money might represent an unacceptable risk, the Employer may also require an advance payment bond. In the latter case, additional attention must be paid in completing the Contract Data to include a description of the form of the advance payment bond required[70] and the type of surety[71] that will be acceptable.

Secondary Option X15: Limitation of the Contractor's liability for his design to reasonable skill and care

This secondary option is a significant one for architects, especially those who regularly work for design and build contractors.

Essentially, the position on design liability under English law is different from that under other jurisdictions, in that 'reasonable skill and care' is an obligation peculiar to common law. The default under most jurisdictions is 'fitness for purpose' and because NEC3 is designed to be operable under any jurisdiction, an active choice has to be made to limit liability to 'reasonable skill and care'. If the Works Information is drafted in clear enough terms, that limitation of liability can legitimately be made in the Works Information. However, by incorporating Secondary Option X15, the standard of care can be globally limited, which in many cases may be preferable.

Certainly, an architect contemplating engagement within a design and build procurement route by contractors who are themselves under an NEC3 main contract would do well to ask whether Secondary Option X15 has been incorporated!

---

69. Stipulated in the Contract Data.
70. To be stated in the Works Information.
71. The Project Manager has to accept the bank or insurer providing the Option X14 advance payment bond.

Secondary Option X16: Retention

[Not used with main option F]

It may come as a slight surprise to architects that retention is an optional concept under NEC3. It behoves us perhaps to reconsider the intended purpose of retention, in that there are apparent instances of it being abused, more than used, under some standard form contracts.

Retention is generally accepted to serve a useful function in incentivising contractors to return to site to deal with the eventuality of any defects that manifest themselves post-completion. Under some standard form contracts, it is also often used as leverage to ensure that contractors continue to work on elements of a building that were manifestly incomplete or defective when completion was certified in order to give access to an employer. In either scenario, retention that is deducted from the outset of a project is a fairly blunt instrument with which to control post-completion quality, and in any case tends to push contractors towards negative cash flow.

In contemplating NEC3, there is a need to look at retention in the context of partnering principles and incentivisation. Returning to the carrot and stick analogy, it is arguable that retention has always been used as a stick, not a carrot. Not only are sticks inherently dangerous in the arena of partnering, but using a stick from the outset of the contract to tackle a potential post-completion issue seems perverse. NEC3 offers two alternative approaches. First, there is the approach of deciding that other contractual provisions can provide adequate protection from potential defects and therefore the retention Secondary Option X16 is not necessary. Second, where it is decided that retention is necessary in principle, Secondary Option X16 envisages that it will not be deducted from the outset, but only from a point when the cumulative value of the works has reached a certain value, i.e. the so-called 'retention free amount'.[72] Only after this value has been reached, which typically would be shortly before Completion, will retention be deducted, which in practice significantly reduces the period during which the Contractor has to finance the retention sum, without reducing the post-completion protection to the Employer.

This secondary option is not used with main option F, on the policy principle that retention is inappropriate to projects with predominantly subcontracted work.

Secondary Option X17: Low performance damages

This particular secondary option is unlikely to apply in the context of a building project. It is primarily intended for projects that encompass items or installations for which it is not simply a case of either they work or they do not: it provides protection to the Employer in the event that the installation does not work quite as well as it should! In practice, Secondary Option X17 will provide useful protection to employers on projects such as industrial or processing plants where the designed output may not be fully achieved, either temporarily or permanently.

In practice, this secondary option would also protect the Contractor on certain types of project: a defect causing 'low performance' could be accepted under the terms of a contract incorporating Secondary Option X17, rather than having to be treated as a breach of contract without Secondary Option X17.

---

72. To be stated in the Contract Data.

Secondary Option X18: Limitation of liability

This secondary option was a new addition to the NEC on the publication of NEC3. It is probably fair to construe the addition as a policy decision based on consumer demand to have the facility to cap liability, irrespective of the type of project and contract value.

Certainly, on most building projects being carried out under English law, there is a perceptible trend to limit liability in some manner. The reason this appears as a secondary option under NEC3, rather than within the core clauses, is that the contract flexibility is of paramount importance, and it is not desirable under any jurisdiction to have core clauses which might get struck out. Secondary Option X18 is certainly one of the secondary options that architects should discuss particularly carefully with their clients before any decision is made regarding its incorporation or otherwise. In the case of contractor negotiations, it is prudent to consider discussing the inclusion of Secondary Option X18 with the potential contractors.

Again, in the context of a design and build procurement route under an NEC3 main contract, an architect employed by the Contractor would sensibly wish to see Secondary Option X18 incorporated, as liabilities should relate to insurance cover[73] and no architect is going to carry professional indemnity insurance with limitless cover.

[Note: Secondary Option X19 is not used]

Secondary Option X20: Key Performance Indicators

[Not used in conjunction with Secondary Option X12]

The only reason why Secondary Option X20 should not be used with Secondary Option X12 is that Secondary Option X12 potentially offers an even more sophisticated approach to Key Performance Indicators, linked into incentivisation. These two secondary options are therefore designed to be used on an either/or basis, not simultaneously.

Key Performance Indicators, or KPIs, as they are now commonly known, have become a feature of many contracts where a partnering ethos is being encouraged. Their role is essentially to assist in benchmarking relative performance in specific areas within a construction project. A number of M4I[74] demonstration projects have been used to measure and monitor such performance and NEC was the contract of choice for many of those projects.

Secondary Option X20 is intended to provide a relatively simple contractual basis upon which performance targets can be stated, measured and monitored.

[Note: Secondary Option Y(UK)1 is not used]

---

73. Secondary Option clause X18.3.
74. Movement for Innovation, formed in 1998 to implement the recommendations of the Egan Report; joined Constructing Excellence in 2004.

Secondary Option Y(UK)2: The Housing Grants, Construction and Regeneration Act 1996

[Only to be used on UK projects where the Act applies]

The naming of Secondary Option Y(UK)2 is an example of the principle of having secondary options that will only ever be contemplated under certain jurisdictions as a direct response to national legislation.

Secondary Option Y(UK)2 relates specifically to legislation that extends to England and Wales and where the relevant part of that legislation also extends to Scotland.[75] NEC3 differs from the second edition of NEC in that adjudication is no longer dealt with as part of Secondary Option Y(UK)2 (see *Dispute resolution options*, page 41). The purpose of Secondary Option Y(UK)2 under NEC3 is solely to ensure that the payment provisions of the legislation are complied with. It therefore follows that the contract for any project in England, Wales or Scotland which comes under the definition of a 'construction contract'[76] should have Secondary Option Y(UK)2 incorporated.

Irrespective of the specific use of NEC3, architects advising clients will need to be familiar with the project types that will be deemed exceptions[77] to the definition of a construction contract and where the payment provisions of the legislation therefore need not be complied with; i.e. in the case of NEC3, the projects which do not require Secondary Option Y(UK)2 to be incorporated.

Secondary Option Y(UK)3: The Contracts (Rights of Third Parties) Act 1999

[Only to be used on UK projects where required]

Most UK-based architects will be familiar with the common advice to exclude the operation of the Contracts (Rights of Third Parties) Act 1999, because the legislation may be contracted out of.

Secondary Option Y(UK)3 can be seen as a slightly more subtle approach. The legislation can be contracted out of entirely by incorporating Secondary Option Y(UK)3 and by remaining silent as to any third party identity. However, by naming a particular third party, or class of third party, in the Contract Data, it is possible to allow the Act to apply in a specifically controlled manner. In practice, on building projects where third parties – such as funders or tenants – require rights, this approach may be preferable to having a number of specially drafted collateral warranties.

It is not that NEC3 per se alters the decision-making process in relation to whether or not to allow either collateral warranties or invocation of the Act; it is merely that Secondary Option Y(UK)3 facilitates the practical process where a decision has been made to either completely exclude or specifically invoke the Act.

Secondary Option Z: Additional conditions of contract

Any so-called 'Z clause', should be very carefully considered and, if strictly necessary, it should be drafted in a style that is compatible with the drafting of NEC3.

The status of a Z clause is that it *augments* the other contract clauses; it should not purport to *amend* them.

---

75. Part II of the Housing Grants, Construction and Regeneration Act 1996.
76. Section 104, Part II of the Housing Grants, Construction and Regeneration Act 1996.
77. Sections 105, 106 and 107, Part II of the Housing Grants, Construction and Regeneration Act 1996 and the Construction Contracts (England and Wales) Exclusion Order 1998.

There is a strong argument that Z clauses should only be used if genuinely necessary. In the early days of NEC contracts there were many examples of copious drafting of Z clauses, much of which was superfluous and some of which was downright dangerous, in that it either confused the meaning of core clauses or sought to change that meaning without necessarily dealing with the consequences of an isolated change. Such overzealous drafting appears to have diminished significantly, no doubt as a result of the now widespread use of NEC contracts and an ever-improving understanding of them.

Nevertheless, architects should remain vigilant for unnecessary Z clauses, which could creep in as a result of clients seeking legal advice from lawyers who are not entirely familiar with NEC. For reasons of democracy and to move projects forward, there might conceivably be times where letting a superfluous Z clause remain is a reasonable course of action, in that it is very unlikely to be harmful. However, if an architect or their client is unlucky enough to be presented with a long list of Z clauses that appear to amend core clauses, they must resist! A good clue when checking for such dangerous clauses is if the drafting style of Z clauses appears to be old fashioned in comparison with that of the NEC3 standard clauses. This would suggest that a lawyer, quantity surveyor or even an ill-advised architect has returned to the comfortable familiarity of older style standard form contract drafting, possibly having found the absence of such drafting in NEC3 somewhat unnerving.

This may be seen as a controversial point; however, new methods in any sphere can be controversial. This book will hopefully help the reader to form an unequivocal view as to whether NEC3 is a desirable step forwards. Given that society as a whole is made up of people who embrace change and people who resist change, a little self-analysis may be helpful. Architects' training is certainly based on the principle of being competent in designing and managing change, so perhaps architects are particularly well placed to assess the pros and cons of NEC3 itself and, the desirability – or otherwise – of Z clauses for an individual building contract.

Dispute resolution options

The evolution of the NEC dispute resolution option clauses has to be seen in the light of the history of adjudication in the UK relative to the drafting of the NEC. Adjudication as an idea has been around for some time and in its earliest guise was never intended to do more than put roughly the right amount of money in the right person's pocket at roughly the right time. Adjudication was incorporated into the NEC from the outset, initially within core clause Section 9. It was intended to operate as a contractual procedure where either party or both parties felt that their own ability to resolve a disagreement amicably was overstretched. The intention under NEC contracts has always been for the adjudicator to be named in advance, being available to act as and when needed. In the early days of NEC, it is no exaggeration to state that the adjudicator was seen simply as an extension to the parties' acting 'in a spirit of mutual trust and co-operation'. It was foreseeable that the parties might hit a stumbling block in the operation of the contract and might disagree on the appropriate course of action; the adjudicator was there to assist in such a situation. In view of the adjudicator's early involvement by being named in the contract, there was a reasonable expectation that the adjudicator would be familiar in general terms with the project and the contract and would therefore be able to make a judgement on an individual disagreement relatively quickly and easily.

It has been said retrospectively that when Part II of the Construction Act[78] came into force on 1 May 1998 it hijacked adjudication as the NEC knew it. This perception stems from the formality that statutory adjudication has engendered; for example, it is now common for contracting parties to have legal representation. Such formality is in stark contrast to the initial NEC intentions, which were simply pragmatic and provided the contracting parties with impartial assistance in resolving a dispute that they had not managed to resolve unaided.

All the standard form drafting bodies were apparently somewhat challenged by the introduction of this legislation as it was a relatively rare example under English law of the phenomenon of legislation interfering with the principle of freedom of contract. This phenomenon has increased somewhat since;[79] however, it is still surprising to some construction professionals and their clients that the Construction Act is mandatory, i.e. cannot be contracted out of. There was considerable debate, both at the time and subsequently, over the principle of Act compliance and the need to amend standard form contracts to become compliant with the Act in order to avoid the Scheme being operated by default.

Opinions were divided over the extent to which legislation should drive standard form drafting and at the time NEC was unusual among the standard form drafting bodies in leaving the Scheme to apply to projects that came under the Construction Act[80] while core clause Section 9 remained the norm for other adjudications. This original decision should be seen in the context of the international operation of NEC contracts and the wish not to include extraneous drafting in the core clause sections. Interestingly for architects, deliberately having the Scheme apply as a default, rather than maintaining Act compliant drafting, has subsequently been embraced by another standard form building contract.[81]

The post-Construction Act status quo was maintained under the NEC second edition for a short time, until the first official legal comment on the NEC contract, specifically the NEC second edition Secondary Option Y(UK)2.[82] The issue essentially revolved around whether the requirement for the issue of a Notice of Dissatisfaction as a precondition for a dispute being deemed to have arisen a minimum of four weeks later constituted a breach of the right conferred under the Construction Act to commence an adjudication 'at any time'.

This case provoked a debate within one of the standard form drafting bodies on a dispute resolution clause with similar drafting to Secondary Option Y(UK)2.[83] As a consequence, when the review of the NEC second edition provisions took place the drafting panel decided to move all adjudication provisions outside both core clause Section 9 and the secondary option clauses. The Construction Act indirectly caused the drafting of a new breed of NEC option clauses, the 'W' options for dispute resolution.

Under NEC3, there are two dispute resolution options, one of which must be chosen.

Option W1

Option W1 is the dispute resolution procedure used unless the United Kingdom Housing Grants, Construction and Regeneration Act 1996 applies. This remains a contractual adjudication, using contractual adjudication procedures.

---

78. The Housing Grants, Construction and Regeneration Act 1996, Part II was brought into force by the Scheme for Construction Contracts (England and Wales) Regulations 1998.
79. E.g. the Contracts (Rights of Third Parties) Act 1999.
80. NEC second edition secondary option Y(UK)2: The Housing Grants, Construction and Regeneration Act 1996.
81. JCT Standard Building Contract 2005 (SBC 05).
82. Judge Toulmin's obiter comments in *John Mowlem & Company PLC* v. *Hydra-Tight & Company PLC (t/a Hevilifts)* 2000.
83. ICE Conditions of Contract, seventh edition, September 1999.

Option W2

Option W2 is the dispute resolution procedure used in the United Kingdom when the Housing Grants, Construction and Regeneration Act 1996 applies. This enables a statutory adjudication, using contractual adjudication procedures in place of the adjudication procedures in the Scheme.

The intention has been to make the language and terminology in Options W1 and W2 as similar as possible, while ensuring that Option W2 is Act compliant. The crucial difference between the two options is that Option W1 still only allows the contracting parties to refer a dispute to the adjudicator after specific notification periods between the contracting parties (as laid out in its Adjudication Table), whereas Option W2 has to allow either contracting party to refer a dispute to the adjudicator *at any time* in order to remain Act compliant.

Contract Data

Role of the Contract Data

The Contract Data is a sophisticated document, defining the project-specific parameters clearly in relation to the generic contract conditions, i.e. the core clauses. The requirement for both Employer and Contractor to prepare Contract Data (Part One and Part Two respectively) ensures parity from the outset and is consistent with the universal reciprocity between parties to any of the NEC family contracts.

Part one: Data provided by the Employer

The principle of project-specific parameters relative to generic contract conditions will be familiar to architects from other standard form building contracts. The dual role of such project-specific parameters is also well-established, i.e. the initial function to define requirements at tender stage and the subsequent function to make the contract operable at construction stage. NEC3 does not deviate from these principles and most architects should find Contract Data Part One fairly self-explanatory.

An area for caution is where the additional items are completed for the chosen main option and for any chosen secondary options, as these are just as important as the entries against the core clause sections. Also, if a large number of secondary options, or if certain option combinations are chosen, particular care is required to complete Contract Data Part One correctly.

Part two: Data provided by the Contractor

The reciprocal requirement for contractors to provide project-specific information at tender/negotiation stage will be less familiar to architects. However, it is easy to see how this is intended to operate and give much greater control over managing projects subsequently.

The key point for architects to note is that in the context of assessing compensation events, the information completed in Contract Data Part Two ensures both objective and foreseeable assessment bases, as well as being contractually binding. In practice, this is likely to make a major contribution to dispute avoidance on many building projects.

Schedule of Cost Components

Role of the Schedule

Possibly the most important point to emphasise about the schedule is that it is not any sort of price list. The word 'component' is key, in that the schedule provides a comprehensive method for breaking down costs into recognisable and objective components.

There are two versions of the schedule, the full and the shorter schedule of cost components:

- **Full Schedule of Cost Components**
  The full version applies with main options C, D and E. It is permissible with these main options to apply the shorter version to compensation events only.

- **Shorter Schedule of Cost Components**
  The shorter version always applies to main options A and B and architects may therefore find that it is worth familiarising themselves with this version first.

Neither schedule applies to main option F.

It takes a little practice to fully understand both of these schedules, but it will become apparent to architects that, whichever schedule applies, the objectivity they are based upon is a major step forward in comparison with assessing costs in a subjective manner.[84]

Both schedules split costs into the following component categories:

- People

- Equipment – note the definition of Equipment covers temporary works (including machinery etc.)[85]

- Plant and Materials – note the definition of Plant covers permanent works[86]

- Charges

- Manufacture and fabrication

- Design

- Insurance.

It is the extent of subdivision within each category which is greater under the full schedule than the shorter schedule.

Defined Cost

As the term implies, cost is not necessarily the same as amount spent, but rather comprises sums which define entitlement to payment under the contract. The definition itself takes place relative to the Schedule of Cost Components; Defined Cost will therefore entitle payment of sums falling under the component categories.

---

84. E.g. on a 'fair and reasonable' basis.
85. Core clause 11.2 (7).
86. Core clause 11.2 (12).

Defined Cost record-keeping requirements vary under the six main options and, clearly, entitlement to payment relies on the required records being available.

Disallowed Cost

The corollary to payment entitlement depending on Defined Cost as recorded under the Schedule of Cost Component categories is that where a cost falls outside those categories it will be disallowed – i.e. Disallowed Cost. Costs will also be designated as Disallowed Cost where records do not justify those costs and in circumstances where contractual procedures have not been followed properly, such as where the Works Information has not been followed or required communications have not taken place. The rules as to when a cost might be classified as Disallowed Cost are to be found in the specific definition of Disallowed Cost given under main options C, D, E and F.

Priced contracts under main options A and B do not recognise Disallowed Cost, as the mechanism for changing the prices is controlled solely by the compensation event procedure.

Works Information

Works Information can be summarised as the entire information a Contractor requires in order to know what to build (and how). The contract definition is as follows:[87]

Works Information is information which either
- specifies and describes the *works* or
- states any constraints on how the *Contractor* Provides the Works

and is either
- in the documents which the Contract Data states it is in or
- in an instruction given in accordance with this contract.

The quality of the design documentation is of paramount importance under NEC3. Some designers are concerned that there is nowhere to hide, although arguably there never should have been. (Even older standard form contracts in their latest versions are introducing greater accountability for information release for construction.)

The NEC does not distinguish between tender documents and contract documents, but instead gives the generic term of Works Information to all design documentation, whether it be drawings, descriptive or performance specifications or schedules.

Architects should ideally treat the designation Works Information simply as a neat receptacle (whether bucket or cardboard box!) in which to meticulously place *all* production information – preferably once and once only, and in the right format and order for ease of comprehension. That is not a definition, as it is not an exclusively NEC-related aim; however, because of the status of the Works Information, NEC3 will be found less forgiving than some standard form contracts if that aim is not pursued.

For the avoidance of doubt, any architect wondering whether and/or where to place an NBS specification or preliminaries in an NEC package should immediately reach for the Works Information. However, such documents need to have been prepared with greater rigour than may be the default norm if they are not to risk acquiring unwanted characteristics.

---

87. Core clause 11.2 (19).

The Works Information is a vital part of the NEC documentation and functionality. Architects need to be very comfortable with the principle of it, in order to ensure that their design information has the intended contractual status. It is also important to acknowledge the status of the Works Information as a live set of documents, which can be changed during the currency of the contract in order to respond to project requirements (see *Change control*, page 57).

Site Information

NEC3 separates the design of the construction from the risks inherent in the context of the construction. Site Information can be summarised as all available information for the Contractor to assess the context of the construction and therefore the risks. The contract definition is as follows:[88]

Site Information is information which
- describes the Site and its surroundings and
- is in the documents which the Contract Data states it is in.

Completeness of Contractor's perception of Commercial Risk

Many commercial risks (e.g. ground conditions) are likely to be greater in the Site Information than in the Works Information. A serious inaccuracy in the Site Information might lead to the Works Information having to be amended, e.g. foundation redesign. A Contractor relies on accurate and complete Works Information and Site Information in order to be able to assess accurately at tender stage the commercial risks inherent in a particular project. It may be advantageous for the Employer to carry the risk of incomplete or inaccurate Site Information, if the unknowns are such that the Contractor would be pricing an unquantifiable risk. Allocation of risk between the parties to a building contract will affect cost – on a similar principle to the cost of insurance being related to the extent of cover.

The Agreement

NEC3 envisages that the contract conditions are incorporated by reference and that the parties to the contract enter into an Agreement which accurately describes the required generic clauses and the project-specific parameters.

It is open to the parties to an NEC3 contract to draw up their Agreement as a bespoke document. This stems from the envisaged flexibility of NEC3, to make it applicable regardless of who will use it, for which project, in which country and under what jurisdiction.

As with all contracts entered into under English law, the parties may execute the Agreement as a simple contract[89] or it may be expressed as a deed.[90]

---

88. Core clause 11.2 (16).
89. Six years' liability under The Limitation Act 1980.
90. Twelve years' liability under The Limitation Act 1980.

3 Contract machinery

The purpose of this chapter is to explore on a pragmatic basis the key areas where NEC3 differs most from old-style standard form contracts. Architects will find these areas decisive in relation to contract administration under NEC3.

People

The players in NEC3 will not be entirely familiar to all new users, as distinct roles have been created to facilitate flexible use of people's skills to suit individual projects and project teams. This section outlines the people in NEC3 and their roles under the contract.

Employer and Contractor

The *Employer* and the *Contractor* are the parties to a *Black Book* NEC3 building contract and are therefore the signatories, as with other construction contracts. The Agreement for signature is drawn up as a bespoke document for each NEC contract, similarly to the Contract Data, in order to take account of project-specific aspects. The *Black Book* is then administered by the Project Manager and the Supervisor.

The term Employer is used across the NEC contract family: e.g. in the NEC3 Short Contract (where the complexity of the project does not warrant contract administration by a Project Manager and a Supervisor) and in the PSC (in the context of engaging consultants).

Project Manager and Supervisor

There is a separation of the time and cost contract administration function from the quality contract administration function within the NEC3 contract, and a potential separation of both of these functions from any pre-contract design. The Project Manager (usually referred to as the PM for short) performs the time and cost contract administration function and may potentially come from any appropriate discipline. On building projects, architects should be well equipped to perform this role, although many quantity surveyors or cost consultants have acted as Project Manager under NEC contracts. The Supervisor performs the quality inspection contract administration function, and again, on building projects, architects should be well equipped to perform this role, although other disciplines, including clerks of work, are capable of taking on the Supervisor role. The key to the Supervisor's correct contract administration will be a good understanding of the Works Information and the ability to assess compliance with it when inspecting the works. Quality is to be assessed relative to the standards stipulated in the Works Information documentation.

In practice, Employers are given the freedom to appoint the appropriate bodies to each of these distinct functions: (designer), Project Manager and Supervisor. It is perfectly possible for one consultant, who may be the architect, to act as lead designer and additionally as both Project Manager and Supervisor, if required. (The identity of the Project Manager and the Supervisor will be stated in Contract Data Part One.)

In the early days of NEC, architects tended to believe that the contract was not for them as it made no mention of the Architect. However, even those standard form contracts that do refer to the Architect are doing so in the Architect's capacity as contract administrator, not as designer, and it therefore follows that NEC is not in any way excluding architects from fulfilling a contract administration role. The roles of Project Manager and Supervisor are deliberately not discipline specific, in order to remain compatible with the notion of NEC contracts themselves not being sector specific.

It is entirely logical that architects will be suitable contract administrators for building projects that are to be built under an NEC3 form of contract. The only decision that needs to be made in order to gain maximum advantage from the flexibility of NEC3 is whether that contract administration would benefit from the separation of the time and cost function and the quality function. In practice, that decision will be influenced both by the procurement route for a particular project and by the preferences and skills of individual architects.

One important aspect of the contract administration roles of both Project Manager and Supervisor is the question of authority. This merits particular attention in the context of architects' training and the customs they have developed over many years of using older standard form contracts.

The authority of the Project Manager

Architects will be very familiar with the concept of impartiality in administering traditional standard form contracts. While this no longer includes a quasi-arbitral role, it nevertheless remains very well established through testing in the courts that the Architect administering a traditional standard form contract has a duty to act impartially and is 'holding the balance' as between the Employer and the Contractor.[91] NEC3 language throughout the contract makes the Project Manager unequivocally the *Employer's* man (or woman), which has led to some debate as to the extent to which the Project Manager has a duty to act fairly. In view of the relatively objective assessment criteria contained in the NEC contract drafting, there seems to have only ever been very limited scope for the Project Manager to unfairly favour the Employer; however, this point received brief judicial consideration[92] (in the context of an amended version of the NEC second edition) and this underlined the logic that the Project Manager should maintain an impartial stance in performing contractual duties, such as assessment and certification.

The authority of the Supervisor

Architects will also be very familiar with the advice given in relation to administering traditional standard form contracts, that the Architect only *inspects* and does not *supervise*. It follows, therefore, that some architects may be reluctant to take on the role of Supervisor for fear of assuming responsibility inferred from the title. This is an example of the lack of transferability of terms between older and newer standard form contracts and the only sensible advice in relation to architects, NEC3 and the title Supervisor is 'fear not'. It is reasonable to expect the authority of the Supervisor to be construed relative to the description of the role within NEC3 and, provided an architect is comfortable with that role, there should be no grounds for concern in an architect being the Supervisor.

---

91. *Sutcliffe* v. *Thackrah* 1974.
92. Mr Justice Jackson's obiter comments in *Costain Ltd & Others* v. *Bechtel Ltd* 2005.

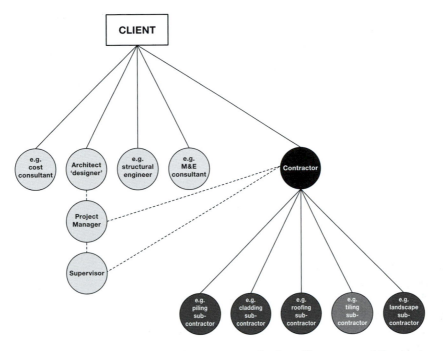

Figure 13 **'Traditional' procurement: architect acts as Project Manager and Supervisor**

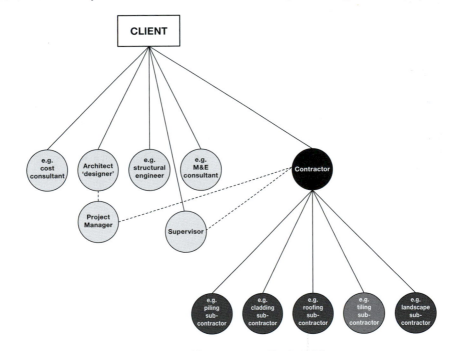

Figure 14 **'Traditional' procurement: architect acts as Project Manager**

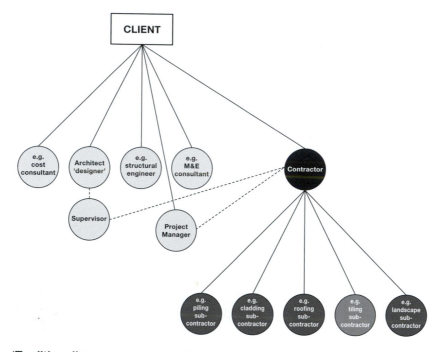

Figure 15   'Traditional' procurement: architect acts as Supervisor

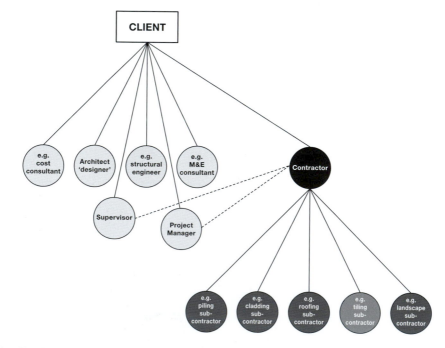

Figure 16   'Traditional' procurement: architect does not administer building contract ('designer' role only)

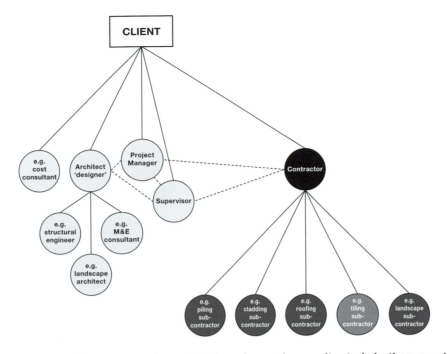

Figure 17 'Traditional' procurement: architect employs subconsultants (whether or not acting as Project Manager/Supervisor)

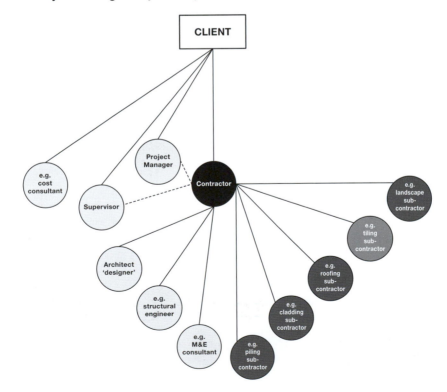

Figure 18 Design and build procurement: architect employed by Contractor

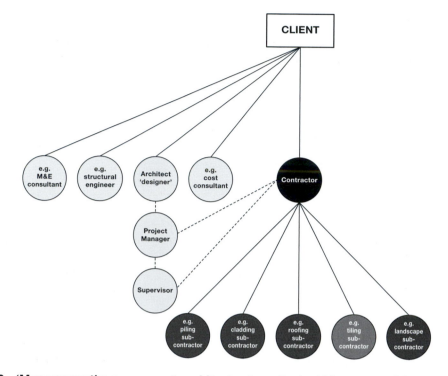

Figure 19 'Management' procurement: architect acts as Project Manager and Supervisor

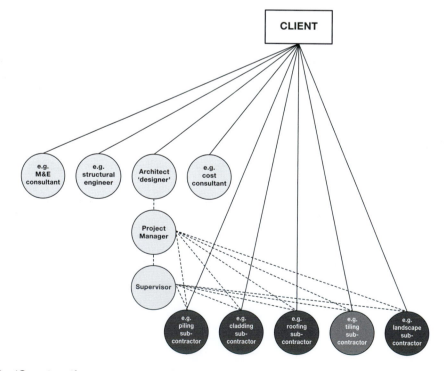

Figure 20 'Construction management' procurement: architect acts as Project Manager and Supervisor

Subcontractor

Subcontractors are all bodies in contract with the Contractor to provide part of the works, whether or not they carry design responsibility, and even if they are not employed under the NEC Subcontract, although the Project Manager has to accept any other conditions of subcontract.

Others

Others are defined in the *Black Book* NEC3 building contract as people who are not the Employer, Project Manager, Supervisor, adjudicator, Contractor or employee, Subcontractor or supplier of the Contractor. (This would in practice include Consultants under a PSC.)

Adjudicator

The adjudicator is the person to whom any crystallised dispute during the contract will be referred in the first instance (after review by the Core Group if Secondary Option X12 is included in the contract) and the person who is empowered to settle such a dispute on an interim binding basis. If either party is dissatisfied with the adjudicator's decision, they may take the dispute afresh to the chosen Tribunal (litigation or arbitration) after completion. (Note the distinction between a statutory and a contractual adjudication.)

Consultant

The Consultant can be a specialist from any discipline who enters into a PSC with the Employer, who in this context can be either the project sponsor or a Contractor in a design and build procurement strategy.

Client

The Client is the project sponsor in partnering relationships where Secondary Option X12 is included in the contract. The distinction between Client and Employer should be noted, as many NEC3 contracts which include Secondary Option X12 may have an Employer who is not the project sponsor. For example, an architect may employ a consulting engineer as a subconsultant under an NEC3 Professional Services Contract that includes Secondary Option X12 – in that instance, the Employer will be distinct from the Client.

Programme

The programming requirements under NEC3 are simultaneously onerous and desirable.

The status of the NEC3 programme is that it is mandatory. The form of the programme is really nothing short of a critical-path-style programme, which needs to be prepared and kept current in order to comply with the NEC3 core clause section 3 requirements.

The function of the NEC3 programme is essentially to integrate the contract obligations with efficient project management.

Pricing and payment

The selected main option clearly has a fundamental impact on the manner in which NEC3 contracts are initially priced and the subsequent procedures that must be operated both in order to make interim payments and to adjust payments in the event of authorised changes. It is key to understand that the defined calculation method for the Price for Work Done to Date (PWDD) varies depending on the main option selected.

The functionality of each main option is described in Chapter 2, but it will also be necessary to look in detail at how the pricing and payment procedures are typically managed on a building project.

Architects acting as Project Manager should note the two distinct actions of assessing the amount due at each assessment date (core clause 50.1) and certifying a payment within one week of each assessment date (core clause 51.1).

Design

Design responsibility

> The *Contractor* designs the parts of the *works* which the Works Information states he is to design.[93]

This deceptively simple core clause is a very powerful tool in terms of legitimate placing of design responsibility. Essentially, it is for the architect to decide exactly which elements of the project should be designed by whom. In practice, this decision-making process requires a clarity of vision in terms of who is best placed to carry that design responsibility and architects should be in a position to exercise their judgement on this in an impartial manner.

The ability to allocate design anywhere between 0% and 100% as between Employer and Contractor without any change in the form of contract or procedures is very advantageous in practice. The only area for caution in this simple but effective approach is in the clarity of explaining both the required design proportion and any cut-off point.

Design submission and acceptance

> The *Contractor* submits the particulars of his design as the Works Information requires to the *Project Manager* for acceptance.
>
> The *Contractor* does not proceed with the relevant work until the *Project Manager* has accepted his design.[94]

'Future' design

Under many conventional standard form contracts, there has developed a culture of allowing relatively important decisions to be made retrospectively relative to contract formation. This is usually driven by a desire to commence the construction phase when the design phase is still incomplete.

---

93. Core clause 21.1.
94. Core clause 21.2.

Given that managing projects in real time is a key objective of NEC3, the contract deliberately omits procedures which allow procrastination. Provisional sums are conspicuous by their absence in NEC3 and this is entirely intentional. In the event of incomplete Consultant design at the point of wishing to appoint the Contractor, the architect or design team has the choice as to whether to postpone entering into the building contract until that design is complete or to legitimately allocate that design responsibility to the Contractor, or a specialist Subcontractor to the Contractor, and to control the quality of that design by means of an appropriate performance specification.[95]

Temporary works design

Architects will be interested to see that there is a mechanism for dealing with temporary works design.[96]

Design liability

The standard of care that is usual for designers practising under English law is 'reasonable skill and care', rather than 'fitness for purpose'. Conventionally, design and build contracts either expressly state a reasonable skill and care obligation, or imply it by specific comparative reference to other designers.[97] The NEC3 core clauses are silent on the subject of design liability and the default liability therefore must be construed as fitness for purpose. This must be understood in the context of the international aims of NEC3 and the peculiarity of reasonable skill and care to common-law jurisdictions.

In practice, the fitness for purpose obligation may be modified by two methods:

- describing the design liability accurately in the Works Information

- invoking Secondary Option X15.[98]

Defects

Defects are the domain of the Supervisor, not the Project Manager, which requires attention to be paid to the distinct role of Supervisor – even if the two roles are being undertaken by the same firm of consultants, and even if those consultants are additionally performing a design role.

A Defect is defined as:[99]

- a part of the works which is not in accordance with the Works Information

  or
- a part of the works designed by the *Contractor* which is not in accordance with the applicable law or the *Contractor's* design which the *Project Manager* has accepted.

Architects will be interested to note the distinction between the *defects date* and the *defects correction period*. The former is the familiar contractual longstop for post-completion defects to be rectified under the contract (without needing to be treated as a breach of contract); the latter is the period within which any individual defect must be corrected, following its notification. In practice, this is a valuable tool for architects to ensure that defects cannot blight the occupation of a new building by being left for

---

95. Documented in the Works Information.
96. Core clause 23.1.
97. E.g. JCT 2005 Design and Build Contract (DB05), Clause 2·17·1.
98. Limitation of the Contractor's liability for his design to reasonable skill and care.
99. Core clause 11.2(5).

long periods before correction. In deciding appropriate periods for individual building projects – to be completed in Contract Data Part One, it is clearly necessary to consider the lead-in times which may be necessary to obtain spare parts etc. in order to correct defects.

Dispute management

Early warning

The first tier of dispute management under NEC3, beyond the obvious informal level of discussion, is the early warning procedure.[100] The intention is that any matter that could affect time, cost or quality issues is notified to the other party for joint resolution. If necessary, an early warning meeting will be held in order to agree on a strategy to remove or mitigate the risk. It should be noted that compensation events are not necessarily early warning matters and that notifying an early warning matter is not inextricably linked with notifying a compensation event.

Adjudication

The second tier of dispute management is resolution by adjudication.

The Tribunal

The final tier of dispute management is by either arbitration or litigation, depending on which Tribunal has been entered into Contract Data Part One.

Communications

Rigour of communication

There are a number of defined forms of communication, in defined directions between specific people, which are intended to be used as clear and unequivocal statements of both the legal and management status of events occurring on the project. Some users have commented that they experience an increase in paperwork with the NEC; this must, however, be seen in the context of the usual large volume of undefined letters on projects under other forms of contract. In practice, most users find that some system of consecutively numbered proformas[101] for each communication type works well, avoiding completely the need for contract administration letters. The discipline of communication following the NEC procedures requires rigour and facilitates clear, objective statements, rather than subjective letters which might be open to interpretation.

Collective responsibility

Many of the obligations to communicate are potentially reciprocal between the parties, e.g. a notification of an early warning can be either from *Project Manager* to *Contractor* or from *Contractor* to *Project Manager*.

Communication types

Architects will be very familiar with instructions and certificates as communications types under building contracts. NEC3 contracts operate additional communication types, with which architects will need to become familiar: assessments, notifications, acceptances and records. See the Appendix for a checklist of communications, by clause number, by type of communication and by initiator.

---

100.   Core clause 16.
101.   Proforma specimens can be found in various publications relating to the NEC and examples are also given in the Appendix (page 89).

Change control

There are some fundamental issues in the context of change control, which can be summarised in the following manner:

- It is pointless to fight change over the lifecycle of a building project; it is inevitable and must therefore be managed.
- Changes over the lifecycle of a project can be few or many and major or minor; their management needs to be appropriate.[102]

NEC3 provides a detailed mechanism for managing change in core clause Section 6: Compensation events. This section, probably the most complicated in the entire NEC3 contract, is critical in terms of enabling efficient project management.

NEC3 adopts a prescriptive approach to change management, which is regarded by some as controversial, but by others as revolutionary.

The compensation event procedure comprises the following:

1. **Definition**

   There is a list of items which are compensation events.[103] This approach will be familiar to architects from other standard form contracts[104] and administering the compensation event procedure will initially be a matter of checking what is happening on a real project against that list.

2. **Notification**

   There is a reciprocal duty for the Project Manager and the Contractor to notify each other of any compensation event when they become aware of it – the detailed obligations are set out in core clause 61.

3. **Quotations**

   The Project Manager must instruct the Contractor to prepare a quotation, or alternative quotations, when the compensation event is instigated on behalf of the Employer, whether the Project Manager or Supervisor simultaneously gives an instruction, or whether a decision to instruct will depend on the outcome of a quotation.[105] The Project Manager must also instruct the Contractor to prepare a quotation for any other compensation event. The timescales both for the Contractor to submit a quotation and for the Project Manager to reply are prescriptive.[106] They can be extended by agreement between the Project Manager and the Contractor,[107] although such agreement should only be based upon genuine necessity.

4. **Assessment**

   Compensation events are assessed relative to Defined Cost and the Accepted Programme and quotations must deal with both time and money. The detailed provisions in core clause 63 must be followed by the Contractor. There are circumstances in which the Project Manager must assess a compensation event – these are governed by the detailed provisions in core clause 64.

5. **Implementation**

   Compensation events are implemented when their time and money implications are fixed. Architects should note that these implications are fixed once and once only and not revisited *even* in the context of a prediction subsequently not transpiring.[108]

---

102.   Engineering projects will typically have relatively few, but major changes; building projects are likely to have relatively many, but minor changes.
103.   Core clause 60.1.
104.   E.g. relevant events under JCT 05.
105.   Core clause 61.1.
106.   Core clause 62.3.
107.   Core clause 62.5.
108.   Core clause 65.2.

Time and money are inextricably linked through the programme and Defined Cost.

Architects may consider the compensation event procedure to be particularly challenging; however, it is worth remembering that conventional standard form contracts have not avoided the need to manage change, they have simply pushed much of the work to the post-completion phase. NEC3 requires contemporaneous change management effort; the reward is to the whole project team in terms of certainty of outcome and avoidance of potential post-completion disputes.

Time-barring

The compensation event procedure includes temporal obligations with respect to change management that are both reciprocal and onerous. The potential time and money rights of the parties in relation to change can be time-barred if the contractual timescales are not followed. Specifically, if the following actions which confer those time and money rights are not taken within the specified time periods, then those rights are extinguished:

- The Contractor must notify a compensation event within eight weeks of becoming aware of it – it is a large carrot to notify a compensation event on time if the right to it can be extinguished after eight weeks.[109]

- The Project Manager must notify the Contractor within two weeks of receipt if any event is considered not to be a compensation event – it is an equally large carrot to check a compensation event on time if it is deemed to be accepted after two weeks by default, i.e. if it is not proactively rejected if it is considered incorrect.[110]

The purpose of such time-barring is to effectively incentivise the parties to perform efficiently and deal with compensation events as they arise. This is a critically important objective of NEC3 in dealing with change contemporaneously and not leaving it for a final account debate.

Completion

Definition of completion

The first thing to clarify with completion under NEC3 is that there is no 'practical completion' as found under many other standard form building contracts. The default position is therefore that Completion occurs when the project is actually finished.

The default position can be modified as a result of the content of the Works Information and architects should carefully consider the project programme in order to determine whether anything could, or should, be left until after Completion – e.g. soft landscaping which ought to take place during a planting season.

Take over

NEC3 provides a mechanism for the Employer to use parts of the works prior to Completion, as well as a requirement for the Employer to take over the works after Completion.[111] It is open to the parties to regulate the relationship between Completion and the Completion Date at the outset by stating requirements in the Contract Data.

---

109.   Core clause 61.3.
110.   Core clause 61.4.
111.   Core clause 35.

4 Collaborative working with NEC3

Professional services

Relationship to the building contract

In order to benefit significantly from the integrated project management principles of NEC3, it will be necessary to bring the NEC3 family together to work as a collaborative team. The first step in this direction is the NEC3 Professional Services Contract (PSC; the *Orange Book*). There is parity between the PSC *Orange Book* and the NEC3 *Black Book* (Figure 21), such that the contracts operate in a back-to-back manner, with differences only in the conventions applicable to Consultants' and Contractors' respective roles. The *Orange Book* shares the *Black Book*'s philosophy, so most of the lessons learnt in the context of an NEC3 building contract will be equally applicable to the PSC, including the all-important structure.

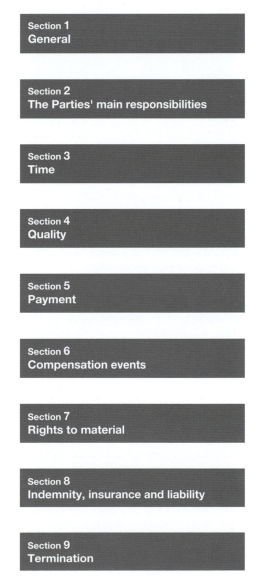

Section 1
General

Section 2
The Parties' main responsibilities

Section 3
Time

Section 4
Quality

Section 5
Payment

Section 6
Compensation events

Section 7
Rights to material

Section 8
Indemnity, insurance and liability

Section 9
Termination

Figure 21   PSC core clauses

The following key points should be considered with respect to the PSC.

Application of the PSC for any discipline of Consultant

All types of professional services can be successfully performed by Consultants appointed under the PSC. On projects requiring a number of different Consultants, having everyone signed up on the same basis can be of enormous benefit.

Cultural and procedural change

To operate the PSC successfully and reap its rewards, a cultural shift in perspective is required. If staff cling to old habits and are suspicious of new ideas then many of the benefits of the PSC will never be realised. However, rapid change and new technologies are now a part of life and learning a new system – one which is truly new, rather than just new to the user – means that bad habits cannot develop. The objectivity of the PSC also makes it unlikely to be open to many varying interpretations.

The PSC encourages, even demands, better documentation and more efficient management skills. It is often said that there is 'nowhere left to hide'; if the procedures are ignored or incorrectly applied, however, the error is virtually immediate and can therefore be rectified for the future, rather than potentially handicapping the project. If a party persistently applies the procedures incorrectly, or even fails to apply them at all, at least a clear breach becomes apparent, rather than there being an argument over semantics. It clearly takes both parties to 'act in a spirit of mutual trust and co-operation'!

Responsibility, authority and people organisation

The PSC necessitates a clear line of both delegated responsibility and authority. Failing to provide this would make it unlikely that decisions could be reached within the required timescales. Many consultancy organisations train staff on trial projects under the PSC, which can be measured against projects that have been carried out under conventional appointment documents.

Using NEC3 may be easier if there is a clear understanding of people's functions during pre-contract, post-contract and post-completion stages, which may overlap.

Multidisciplinary and project-specific nature of the Scope

The Scope is the *Orange Book*'s equivalent of the *Black Book*'s Works Information. The contract definition is as follows:[112]

The Scope is information which either
- specifies and describes the *services* or
- states any constraints on how the *Consultant* Provides the Services

---

The Scope should be arrived at on the basis of building up an appropriate range of services relative to a particular Consultant's discipline and required input on a particular project. While any formulaic tendencies, based on ticking 'standard services', should ideally be avoided, there is no difficulty in using discipline-specific conventions as a framework for the Scope.

---

112.   PSC core clause 11.2 (11).

For example, the RIBA Plan of Work can be used as the framework for defining the range of services required from an architect on a particular project – however, the actual tasks to be performed under each work stage should be carefully considered and documented in the Scope.

If this approach is taken in arriving at the Scope for each Consultant, it should ensure that there are no gaps or overlaps in the total range of Consultants' services performed on a project, providing a seamless back-to-back range of professional services for a project.

Consultant designers in particular have conventionally worked to standard services schedules, which do not always assist clients in understanding the complexity of work being undertaken. One of the benefits of the PSC is that it encourages a distinction between the tasks being performed and the deliverables resulting from such activities, which can be seen as equally helpful to both Consultants and Employers.

The documentation of the services to be provided under a PSC takes an appropriate form relative to the discipline and the project, irrespective of whether the Employer of the Consultant has conventional client, contractor or 'lead' consultant status.

No conventional percentage fee basis

While conventional standard form professional services contracts have been largely based on a percentage fee calculation and resource-based fee calculations can still be seen as rare in some sectors, the PSC offers considerably more flexibility and accuracy in fee calculation through its main options. Many building clients will no longer tolerate a fee basis predicated on the principle of fees increasing with construction costs – which can be seen as almost a disincentive for consultants to be proactive in keeping projects within a set budget.

Architects will be interested in the fee bases offered under the PSC payment mechanisms (Figure 22).

Main Option **A**
Priced contract with activity schedule

Main Option **C**
Target contract

Main Option **E**
Time based contract

Main Option **G**
Term contract

Figure 22   PSC main option clauses

Fine tuning a PSC Consultant's role

In addition to the complementary main option payment mechanisms, there is also parity in the secondary options as between the PSC *Orange Book* and the NEC3 *Black Book*, with adjustments to recognise the PSC Consultant's role (Figure 23).

Secondary Option **X1**
Price adjustment for inflation

Secondary Option **X2**
Changes in the law

Secondary Option **X3**
Multiple currencies

Secondary Option **X4**
Parent company guarantee

Secondary Option **X5**
Sectional Completion

Secondary Option **X6**
Bonus for early Completion

Secondary Option **X7**
Delay damages

Secondary Option **X8**
Collateral warranty agreements

Secondary Option **X9**
Transfer of rights

Secondary Option **X10**
Employer's Agent

Secondary Option **X11**
Termination by the Employer

Secondary Option **X12**
Partnering

Secondary Option **X13**
Performance bond

Note:
Options X14–X17 are not used in the *Orange Book*

Secondary Option **X18**
Limitation of liability

Note:
Option X19 is not used in the *Orange Book*

Secondary Option **X20**
Key Performance Indicators

Secondary Option **Y(UK)2**
The Housing Grants, Construction and Regeneration Act 1996

Note:
Jurisdiction specific

Secondary Option **Y(UK)3**
The Contracts (Rights of Third Parties) Act 1999

Secondary Option **Z**
Additional conditions of contract

Figure 23   PSC secondary option clauses

Subcontracting

The next step in the direction of the integrated project management principles of NEC3 is the NEC3 Subcontract (the *Purple Book*). Again, there is parity between the NEC3 *Purple Book* and the NEC3 *Black Book*, such that the contracts operate in a back-to-back manner, with the difference in the step down, so that the Employer becomes the Contractor, and the Contractor the Subcontractor. Under the NEC3 Subcontract conditions, the Contractor manages the time, cost and quality subcontract administration and, in the context of quality matters, there is recognition of both the Employer's and the Supervisor's status under the NEC3 *Black Book*.[113] The now familiar NEC3 structure is maintained.

The NEC3 *Purple Book* main option clauses mirror those of the NEC3 *Black Book*, with the exception of the management contract option (*Black Book* Option F).

A critical point for architects who have attempted to manage subcontract risk to clients under older style standard form contracts or subcontracts is the clarity with which such risk is placed on the Contractor under the NEC3 *Black Book*:[114]

> If the *Contractor* subcontracts work, he is responsible for Providing the Works as if he had not subcontracted. This contract applies as if a Subcontractor's employees and equipment were the *Contractor's*.

Subcontracting under NEC3 will sensibly be carried out under either the *Purple Book* subcontract, or, in instances where the subcontracted works are of low complexity, the NEC3 Short Subcontract (the *Turquoise Book*).[115] Indeed, the NEC3 *Black Book* foresees an NEC contract as the default for all subcontracts, unless agreed otherwise:[116]

> The *Contractor* submits the proposed conditions of contract for each subcontract to the *Project Manager* for acceptance unless
> - an NEC contract is proposed or
> - the *Project Manager* has agreed that no submission is required.

The NEC3 *Purple Book* secondary option clauses mirror those of the NEC3 *Black Book* entirely.

Project profiles

It is extremely important in using NEC3 to its best advantage to properly analyse the profiles of individual projects. Such analysis needs to extend beyond the essential procurement strategy and encompass an assessment of participating organisations and the staff employed within them. It would be naïve to expect truly collaborative working between organisations to succeed without considering the people who are expected to collectively make it happen – personalities matter!

Architects are often in a pivotal position with regard to fostering collaboration. This position results partly from the leading role architects may take at the outset of projects, including advising clients on the need for other consultants, and partly from an expectation that most architects can offer excellent communication skills.

---

113.   NEC3 Subcontract core clause 40.
114.   NEC3 *Black Book* core clause 26.1.
115.   Subcontract equivalent to the NEC3 Short Contract.
116.   NEC3 *Black Book* core clause 26.3.

Truly collaborative working requires a partnering-style contract such as NEC3 as a prerequisite for success; however, it would be a fallacy to assume that merely choosing NEC3 as a contractual basis offers any guarantee of success. The people involved in a particular project have to buy into the contractual ethos for a project to be run successfully on a collaborative basis. Just as highly motivated project teams can achieve some degree of collaboration *in spite of* adversarial contract conditions, it follows that unwilling team members can fall out and jeopardise a project *even with* co-operative contract conditions.

Partnering

Partnering as a concept has been recognised in the building industry for some time – essentially the idea of putting the success of the project at the forefront of all parties' goals. Partnering has historically had more than one guise. In its simplest form, partnering has been an intuitive process between project team members (with co-operative personalities). As a more conscious decision, project teams have volunteered to partner by adding a non-binding partnering charter to their (often still adversarial) contract conditions.[117] In its most powerful form, partnering has become mandatory, based on an obligation to work co-operatively in a binding contract. It is this latter model to which NEC3 belongs (Figure 24).

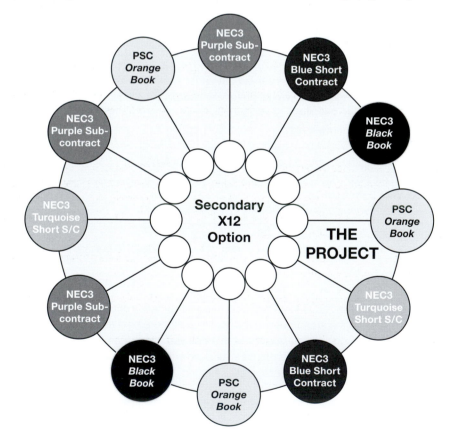

Figure 24   NEC3 partnering

117.   E.g. JCT 98 Practice Note 4 (2001, RIBA Publications).

The CIC Task Force report and the NEC response

In 2000, the Construction Industry Council (CIC) published the findings of its multidisciplinary Task Force research into partnering and provided a possible methodology for contractual partnering.[118] This included model heads of terms, for guidance to the construction industry.[119] The NEC Panel then carried out a review of NEC's compliance with the CIC guide and decided to retain the family structure of bi-party NEC contracts, including the core clauses, main option and secondary option clauses, as it was considered that the NEC family already incorporated most of the objectives of the CIC Guide. In addition, it was decided that a more formal layer of partnering rights and obligations should be added to NEC at secondary option level. The *'White Book'* consultative version of the NEC Partnering Option X12 was published as a supplementary NEC document in September 2000, followed by the first edition in June 2001. Option X12 was incorporated into the main secondary option documentation on publication of NEC3 in 2005.

Extent of partnering

Secondary Option X12 maintains the flexibility of bi-party contracts, but allows specific aspects of partnering to become a contractual obligation if and when required. Contractual partnering arrangements can be tailored to suit both project and people requirements:

- bi-party partnering – requires an NEC contract

- multi-party partnering – requires NEC contracts including Secondary Option X12

- multi-project partnering – requires an NEC contract or series of NEC contracts and can include Secondary Option X12 where multi-party partnering relationships are desired.

Structure and status

Secondary Option X12 sits at secondary option level within the NEC 'pick and mix' framework and is incorporated in exactly the same way as other secondary options. It will be incorporated into as many bi-party contracts as required, which in practice will be the NEC3 contacts between all the key participants in a project. In comparing Secondary Option X12 with other standard form contract approaches to partnering, architects should note the following:

- Option X12 is not a stand-alone contract; it is predicated on an NEC3 family 'base' contract – NEC3 *Black Book*, Subcontract, PSC etc.

- Option X12 does not create a multi-party contract; all Partners share common bi-party rights and obligations.

- Option X12 does not create a legal partnership across bi-party contracts.

---

118.   CIC (2000) *A Guide to Project Team Partnering*, London.
119.   Upon which the partnering contract PPC2000 was subsequently based.

Secondary Option X12 people definitions and scope of application

There are some additional definitions in Secondary Option X12 to become familiar with:

- Client: project sponsor and Employer under some bi-party contracts

- Partner: any team member with Secondary Option X12 in their bi-party NEC contract

- Core Group: group of key partners.

Secondary Option X12 can be incorporated at any level in the supply chain; the contribution made by a Partner is more important than their size.

The contractual partnering relationship commences with the first bi-party NEC family contract that includes Secondary Option X12.

There is provision for Partners to join and leave at appropriate stages of a project or series of projects.

Implementation of Secondary Option X12 documents

The Schedule of Partners is maintained by the Core Group.

The Secondary Option X12 Contract Data identifies the Client and their objective.

The Partnering Information should contain only information which is relevant to all bi-party contracts, i.e. it must be common and not vary across the Partners' contracts.

In order to achieve the required commonality in the Partnering Information, architects should ensure that in compiling the Works Information for a building contract and the Scope for a professional services contract where Secondary Option X12 is to be incorporated in the contract conditions, the drafting is done on a side-by-side basis.

Partners' management responsibilities

Secondary Option X12 creates additional rights and obligations to assist in managing the relationship between Partners. The intended live nature of the Partnering Information necessitates continuous review relative to both the Client's objective and the other Partners' objectives.

There is an important role for the Core Group in both preventive dispute avoidance and as the first tier of a problem-solving hierarchy. Formal dispute resolution and legal remedies are consciously left within the discrete bi-party contracts. This is based on the principle that the potential embarrassment of having to pass a dispute up the supply chain and back down again – to the certain knowledge of the ultimate Client – acts as an active incentive to most bi-party contract parties to resolve their differences amicably. The ultimate sanction for failing to act co-operatively remains, of course, exclusion from future partnering projects.

Secondary Option X12: Partnering subclauses

X12.1 – Actions

The intention is to achieve the Client's objective as stated in the Option X12 Contract Data and the other Partners' objectives as stated in the Schedule of Partners.

The Partners select the Core Group and each nominates a representative.

The Core Group's decision-making remit is stated in the Partnering Information. It works democratically and will normally be led by the Client's representative.

The Core Group maintains the Schedule of Partners and Schedule of Core Group Members throughout the project.

X12.2 – Identified and defined terms

Partners are named in the Schedule of Partners and include the Client.

Own Contract means the bi-party contract between two Partners incorporating Option X12.

The Core Group is the listed group of Partners who will steer the partnering relationships on the project.

Partnering Information specifies how the Partners work together.

Key Performance Indicator targets are stated in the Schedule of Partners.

X12.3 – Working together

Collaborative team working is required as stated in the Partnering Information, in a 'spirit of mutual trust and co-operation'.

Allowance is made for reciprocal provision of Partners' information.

There is provision for each Partner to give early warning of matters affecting other Partners' objectives.

The Partners' contributions are co-ordinated by the Core Group in the form of a timetable, which is incorporated into each Partner's Own Contract programme.

X12.4 – Incentives

Performance of the partnering team, a group of Partners or an individual Partner can be rewarded where a target stated for a Key Performance Indicator is achieved or improved upon.

A final point which architects and their clients will note when comparing partnering methodologies and standard form partnering style contracts is that Secondary Option X12 does not envisage the necessity for an externally appointed partnering advisor. The key reason for such a role not being considered necessary is that individual contracting partners maintain their autonomy with Secondary Option X12, rather than effectively joining an overarching entity, as would be the case were a multi-party contract created.

Framework agreements

Project-specific emphasis

The flexibility of the NEC family allows emphasis to be placed on project-specific solutions. Particularly in the context of long-term relationships and partnering, the NEC family is ideally suited to being used as the basis for an umbrella framework agreement, with subsidiary 'call-off' orders. The precise manner in which this is done will depend on the nature of project requirements and the consequential choices of NEC3 family contracts.

Many architects have gained experience of framework agreements in the context of EU-derived legislation[120] concerning publicly funded – in whole or in part – construction projects. Such framework agreements may well have been contractually complex and may have involved bespoke drafting. One of the fallacies that seemed to surround framework agreements using NEC contracts in the early years of NEC was the apparent presumption that the NEC contracts were invoked at a secondary level, underneath a bespoke umbrella contract. This seems to have had no compelling legal or management basis, but rather to have been a hangover from the manner in which older style standard form contracts might be linked together to form a more collaborative framework agreement. A more successful model in the context of NEC would seem to be to capitalise on the back-to-back drafting and introduce an NEC3 contract as the head framework agreement, with further NEC3 contracts nested into it to deal with individual contractual requirements, whether they be on a task-by-task or project-by-project basis.

A number of relatively high-profile project programmes were developed during the currency of the NEC second edition, procured on the basis of framework agreements predicated on NEC contracts. A public sector example would be one of the NHS procurement programmes for new hospital buildings.[121] A private sector example would be a nationwide expansion of a mobile phone network through construction of additional masts.[122]

NEC3 Framework Contract

The NEC3 Framework Contract was a new addition to the NEC family when the third edition was published in 2005. It achieves a greater clarity in recognising the potential for many project programmes to continue to be procured on the basis of NEC3 framework contracts, with various NEC3 contracts nested into them.

Term services

The NEC3 Term Service Contract (TSC) is of particular interest in the context of whole-life and maintenance contracts. Where appropriate, suppliers can be appointed under the TSC, nested into the NEC3 Framework Contract.

---

120.   Public Contracts Regulations 2006.
121.   NHS ProCure 21 Programme – based on an NEC main option C contract strategy.
122.   Vodafone – based on an NEC Short Contract strategy.

Management systems

Paperless methods

The corollary to logical and efficient communications under NEC3 contracts is that they lend themselves to being managed under a smart IT system. It is entirely feasible to monitor periods of reply for a variety of communications on a project by means of computerised management systems, which will alert users to periods which are about to expire and enable them to meet imminent contractual deadlines. While such management systems would be complete overkill on smaller or more straightforward projects, there is certainly a plausible argument in their favour on larger or more complex projects. This is particularly the case where a number of NEC3 contracts are interrelated, or nested, with consequentially cascading communication timescales. Generic and NEC-specific software has been developed which may assist in managing NEC3 projects, particularly in relation to contractual communications such as notifications.

Many NEC projects have adopted an electronic information-sharing portal to enable the project team members to exchange information, including contractual communications, via an extranet.

The publishers of NEC3 have recently launched official contract management software via two licensed partners.[123]

Support

Architects will probably only want to progress to sophisticated electronic management systems when they have mastered the basics of NEC3 and have honed their communication management skills. Quite a lot of support is available, either directly or indirectly, from the NEC publishing body, Thomas Telford Ltd. There is a well-established group to promote the exchange of information about the NEC in use – the NEC Users' Group, which provides a very useful and transparent forum. There is also a website dedicated to NEC and its wider application, which is an obvious starting point for architects, allied professionals and their clients who are new to NEC3:

- www.neccontract.com

---

123.   4Projects and BIW.

5 International use

Domestic and cross-border

Domestic

Domestic international use means that NEC3 is used by a client based in a country other than the UK for a project within that country, using consultants/subconsultants and contractors/subcontractors who are also based in that country. In that instance, NEC3 would effectively replace any other standard form contract that might be prevalent in that particular country. While this might seem a perverse thing to do in a country which has an established range of standard form contracts, it would still potentially offer an alternative approach by virtue of the ability to marry-up legal and project management requirements. In countries that have historically had little or even no choice of standard form contracts, NEC3 offers a blueprint that could form the basis of a national standard form of contract for that emerging construction economy.

Cross-border

Cross-border international use occurs where NEC3 is used as a neutral contract between parties of different nationalities and where the project may be based either in the same country as one of the parties or in a third country. This type of cross-border use is quite likely on larger projects, for example:

- technically demanding projects where world-class expertise can be drawn from an appropriate country

- projects in developing countries where some of the funding may be in the form of international aid.

These concepts of NEC3 international use have already been explored by international parties from countries as diverse as China, South Africa, Germany, Ethiopia, Ireland and New Zealand. The list of interested countries has grown slowly but steadily and it is to be anticipated that the international use of NEC3 will gradually spread round the world.

Jurisdiction

NEC3 is operable in any jurisdiction, by virtue of the relatively simple device of removing jurisdiction-specific requirements from the core clauses. The choice of jurisdiction is made by entering the appropriate country into the Contract Data (Part One) under the General section:

- The *law of the contract* is the law of...

It would be usual to insert 'England and Wales' for projects in, for example, London.

While it would be unusual, it is theoretically possibly to decide upon a different jurisdiction from that of the country in which the project is situated. For example, if a German bank wished to construct a new office building in London, possibly using some consultants and contractors from Germany, it would be a simple matter of inserting 'Germany' in the Contract Data in order for the jurisdiction of the project to be German law.

Architects should note that there is no default jurisdiction under the contract; it follows, therefore, that there would be serious repercussions from omitting the appropriate country from Contract Data Part One, thereby failing to designate the law of the contract.

Architects working in multi-jurisdictional countries such as the UK or the USA should take particular care in completing this statement in Contract Data Part One. For example, if a Newcastle-based practice were to win a commission in Edinburgh, it would be very important not to just copy the Contract Data entry from a previous project, but rather to have a proper debate with the client and any other interested parties as to whether the applicable law should be the law of England and Wales or the law of Scotland.

This ability to choose jurisdiction is somewhat analogous to the situation in international dispute resolution.[124]

Having established the law of the contract, there is a further key area where architects need to be proactive in ensuring that the national legislative requirements for a project are properly covered. As a direct result of removing jurisdiction-specific requirements from the core clauses, there is no default set of contractual obligations in relation to national legislation, such as CDM[125] compliance requirements on an English project. This may seem slightly irritating to architects who only ever work on projects under a single jurisdiction, as they could be forgiven for considering it an unnecessary additional burden to have to ensure that such legislation is actively referred to.

Quite apart from a real risk of oversight, there is also the risk of not knowing where to add this legislative information to make it as enforceable as if it had been within the generic contract conditions, as it would be in many standard form building contracts. Even for those architects who are not persuaded by this structure – created for the greater good of ease of international use – there is still a viable alternative to simply choosing an alternative, fully nationalised standard form contract. The key is to be found in the all-powerful Works Information: this is the correct place to 'reinstate' the requirement to comply with national legislation. Using the example of CDM compliance requirements on an English project, the statement in the Works Information could be as general as 'The Construction (Design and Management) Regulations 2007 must be complied with'. Equally, there could be detailed stipulations regarding their specific applicability to the project in question, and there could be further contractual requirements outwith the strict remit of the legislation, e.g. there might be a statement that 'All O&M manuals must be provided both in electronic pdf format and as a hard copy on min. 100g paper for the purposes of longevity'.

This is clearly an area that requires careful consideration of appropriate national legislation and there is no getting away from the potential gravity of failing to include certain requirements on individual projects. Some architects may immediately wish to revert to the tried and tested approach of older style standard form building contracts in relation to national legislation. However, there is undoubtedly a counter-argument to that stance: as the trend within English law appears to be moving towards greater influence of legislation over parties' freedom of contract, it behoves architects to get to grips with such legislation affecting construction and to become familiar enough with it to easily incorporate it appropriately into the Works Information for a given project.

---

124.   Conflict of Laws.
125.   Construction (Design and Management) Regulations 2007.

Language and culture

Language

Simple English is used throughout NEC3, avoiding the legalistic language usually associated with construction contracts. Subjective statements are avoided and instead, objective, measurable requirements are stated wherever possible. This approach makes for easier understanding both within the UK and internationally and has generally been welcomed. Some lawyers commented in the early days of the NEC that the use of the present tense throughout resulted in a lack of distinction between statements of fact and statements of legal obligation; in practice, however, this does not appear to have materialised as a tangible difficulty.

Most first-time users of NEC3 will be very struck by the simplicity of the language and will tend to react either positively or negatively – ambivalence is a less likely reaction. Certainly it would be a mistake to confuse simplicity of language with simplicity of purpose or intent and experienced users of NEC3 have learnt that even the shortest sentences are not without effect.

In the context of international use, there is a strong argument for translating the NEC3 documents into other languages. However, in the absence of official translations, the simple English used throughout the documents does assist understanding among those whose mother tongue is not English.

Culture

Cultural diversity is a fascinating aspect of the international use of NEC3, in that its influence can only be established on a trial and error basis. It would never have been possible to assimilate every culture into the drafting of NEC3, as even concentrating on those cultures with a history of using standard form contracts for construction would have required an impossibly large drafting and research body. Instead, NEC3 offers a model that is potentially inclusive of all cultures by means of the following salient devices:

- necessary disconnection of language from culture

- necessary disconnection of jurisdiction from culture

- 'pick and mix' contractual structure, which can be tailored towards cultural precedents and customs.[126]

The relative success of NEC3 in operating within different and new cultures can only be assessed over decades rather than mere years. Countries outside the UK in which NEC3 has been used to a significant extent to date include South Africa and New Zealand. While these countries perhaps do not represent the most radically different cultures in the world relative to England, they are useful examples of successful use of NEC3 in diverse cultures.

---

126.   Including the potential for introducing unique secondary options.

The worldwide history of the evolution of standard form contracts suitable for construction projects cannot be divorced from historical and political events. It is certainly interesting to note how older standard form contracts were initially introduced into other cultures on what could almost be described as a neo-colonial basis.[127] NEC3 goes a very long way in avoiding the imposition of predetermined and possibly inappropriate cultural provisions, particularly those associated with common law principles. Nevertheless, given that the NEC contract was born and bred in England, it has to be acknowledged that some English cultural prejudices are bound to remain, even after the major review leading up to the publication of the third edition, NEC3, in 2005. The international comment on the second edition was not broadly enough based to have raised many cultural issues and it is probably fair to say that some of the potential cultural nuances of NEC3 are yet to be tested. However, to put this into context, even within the confines of the construction industry in England, there are cultural nuances between different professions, such as architects and engineers, and NEC3 copes well in being flexible enough to be tailored to fit novel briefs.

Overall, NEC3 appears unlikely to present any insurmountable cultural challenges wherever it may be used in the world.

---

127.   E.g. Singapore Standard Form of Building Contract, FIDIC Conditions of Contract (Fédération Internationale des Ingénieurs Conseils).

6 In conclusion: decisive features of NEC3

Relative certainty and *carpe diem*

Temporal longstops and avoidance of delay

The rigour of NEC3 communications coupled with the requirement to fix a period for reply in the Contract Data (Part One) effectively eliminate any significant doubt over when any particular contractual issue will be resolved. While NEC3 does make provision for consensual extending of timescales,[128] it is reasonable to assume that such consensus will only be forthcoming when it is genuinely in both contractual parties' interests to allow more time for a particular issue. Experience suggests that where NEC3 is properly operated, it is quite rare for communication time periods to be extended. It is perhaps slightly more common on building projects for compensation event quotation and/or reply periods to be extended; this is because the periods of three and two weeks respectively are generically prescriptive,[129] rather than decided on a project-specific basis. Consequently, depending on the building project in question, it is foreseeable that quotations for compensation events may be more time consuming, whether because of the complexity of an individual compensation event, the involvement of subcontractors, or a plethora of contemporaneous compensation events. In such circumstances, it may well be in both parties' interests to agree in advance to a limited extension of the period in question, although in order to maintain the relative certainty that NEC3 engenders, blanket extensions should never be given.

Real time

One of the most important and potentially beneficial aspects of managing projects under the NEC3 form of contract is the underlying rationale of running projects in real time, without reliance on future negotiations.[130] This can be seen as quite a controversial aspect of NEC3, in that it leaves no room for either procrastination or revisiting difficult decisions. However, this aspect of NEC3 should not be seen as necessarily requiring greater certainty of project objectives at the outset; indeed, NEC3 is predicated on the principle of needing flexibility.

One of the best ways for architects to decide whether NEC3 is something they wish to embrace is possibly to reflect on their own approach to management. Anyone for whom decision-making is preferably an incremental process is likely to find the requirements of NEC3 quite onerous; whereas, anyone who tends towards a holistic approach to making the right decision in all the circumstances at a snapshot in time is much more likely to find NEC3 second nature to them.

---

128.   Core clauses 13.5 & 62.5.
129.   Core clause 62.3.
130.   *Carpe diem (quam minimum credula postero)* – Seize the day (trusting as little as possible in the future). Horace, born 8 December 65 BC.

Consistency

The whole project

The use of NEC contracts to date has seen advantages in appointing everyone within the supply chain for a particular project on an NEC form of contract. These advantages stem from having back-to-back contractual relationships, whether in the context of professional services or in the context of construction. Architects may be used to thinking of the term 'supply chain' as solely relating to contractors and subcontractors; however, given the flexibility of procurement routes that can be supported by NEC3, it is perhaps helpful to get used to the idea that a supply chain includes consultants and subconsultants.

A way of life

Clearly, if NEC3 users get used to and enjoy working collaboratively in such an environment of truly back-to-back contractual relationships, with no gaps or overlaps between the contracts making up the totality of project requirements, it becomes quite appealing to make NEC3 contracts the default for new projects. Architects are in a unique position with their building clients to influence the form of contract proposed for a particular project, in that they are appointed early, if not first, in the process. Of course there will be other knowledgeable and influential players, such as cost consultants, or even contractors, and of course clients themselves will often have strong views about forms of contract. However, in the context of some architects occasionally feeling sidelined over key project management decisions, such as forms of contract, it is worth remembering that knowledge is power. An adequate knowledge of NEC3 will therefore almost certainly put architects in a stronger position to ensure that their designs can be realised reliably and efficiently. It is perhaps also worth remembering that the balance of power in collective knowledge of NEC3 within the construction industry currently rests predominantly outside of the architectural profession and that it is arguably about time that more architects got up to speed. No one is advocating that a particular profession should take sole ownership of NEC3 – it is in essence a democratic form of contract and there are cogent arguments in favour of collaborative ownership, including where appropriate by architects.

Commitment

All or nothing

NEC3 is undoubtedly a standard form of contract that offers the potential to manage projects in a proactive and efficient manner. Indeed, it requires a degree of commitment which is uncommon with other standard form contracts. The contract is too precise to be operated successfully in anything but a completely committed manner.

Of course there are real life examples of where an NEC contract has not been particularly well received and where the parties have not benefited from its use; however, there is strong evidence that such an outcome stems primarily from the way in which the parties approach the contract. It is a form of contract not quite like any of its predecessors and it is certainly not a contract for any ambivalent members of the building industry. If the parties attempt to operate NEC3 in exactly the same way as older standard form contracts, or with only half-hearted embracing of the newer approach, they will almost inevitably fail, simply because such older standard forms are not predicated on the same level of objectivity or precision as NEC3.

No one is particularly likely to be overheard saying they 'quite like NEC3' – they will invariably tend towards a more polarised position. Those who believe in NEC3 are likely to be people with a 'can do', collaborative approach, who like to have a clear structure for managing a project, but who also like a degree of autonomy in making that structure support their particular needs on that project. Anyone who prefers more rigid contractual mechanisms, or who has slightly hierarchical tendencies (possibly getting some satisfaction from thrashing-out any difficulties on a project with an occasional adversarial bunfight!) is likely to be less enamoured of NEC3.

In the context of architects advising their clients on procurement strategies, having analysed contract typology and contract form, it may also be beneficial for the players in a building project to indulge in a little psychoanalysis before finalising their project strategy. Depending on the personalities of the key players on a particular project, they may be more or less well suited to the rigours of proactively managing that project under NEC3 contracts.

While there is no absolute necessity to use NEC3 family contracts across the entire supply chain for a particular project, and there is certainly no prohibition on mixing and matching other standard form contracts with NEC3, it is worth actively considering the sense of this on any particular project. The potential success of a matrix of standard form contracts to cover all the relationships on a building project will be as dependent on the personalities of the parties forming those relationships as it will be on the actual standard form contracts. Experience also suggests that if even one person out of an entire project team is actively uncomfortable with a particular contract, that can be enough to interfere with the operation of that contract, to the point where project success is potentially jeopardised.

The moral of this emphasis on personalities and commitment is that NEC3 should ideally only be used where the key players have in principle both understood and bought into its philosophy and management techniques.

Use patterns

Use of the NEC contract has multiplied exponentially since its inception. The engineering sector within the construction industry has seen its use become the norm on a range of project types, including highways, railways, water supply and other infrastructure areas. The OGC's endorsement of NEC3 in 2005 is important, as other forms of contract are being phased out for government-sponsored works. More recently, the ICE's decision[131] to officially endorse NEC3 as the best practice form of contract for construction projects is also highly significant, marking an 'official' end to the belief in a form of contract rooted in Victorian drafting style and risk allocation.[132]

There is no question that NEC3 has now been embraced wholeheartedly in the public sector for both engineering and building projects. Perhaps the most high-profile and topical project to be undertaken using NEC3 is the multifaceted construction programme for the London 2012 Olympics, where the NEC3 integration of engineering and building requirements in the contract has been replicated in situ. The largest project to use NEC3 to date is Crossrail, also in London – another project requiring integration of many disciplines.

---

131.   August 2009.
132.   ICE Conditions of Contract.

Uptake of the NEC was initially slower in the building sector than the engineering sector, which was probably due to two distinct issues:

- the tendency for engineering works to be on a relatively large scale and sponsored by important, often public sector, patrons, where there is a strong incentive to adopt state-of-the-art best practice, and

- the apparently trivial, but disproportionately significant, subtitling of the NEC in 1995 (the second edition) as the 'Engineering and *construction* contract'.

While the latter was clearly intended to emphasise that the NEC philosophy encompasses more than conventional civil, structural or other engineering works, it was arguably too subtle. Had the subtitle been 'Engineering and *building* contract', it is reasonable to assume that architects and those in their sphere of influence would have picked up on its significance much sooner. Nevertheless, time has taken its course and the building sector has caught up significantly in the use of the NEC form of contract. There are now many buildings standing that were built under the NEC form of contract, whether hospitals, educational establishments, supermarkets or one-off houses. Public sector clients showed the way, but private sector clients are now following.

In the early years of NEC, architects and quantity surveyors/cost consultants tended to be introduced to NEC by their clients, which was perhaps readily understandable given the long history in the building sector of using standard form contracts, traceable back to the Victorian era,[133] and architects' reasonable reluctance to put forward untried or untested methods in any aspect of building. However, a position has been reached where state-of-the-art knowledge in the UK building industry clearly includes the NEC3 form of contract and architects will therefore want to use it of their own volition and be a 'safe pair of hands' in its implementation.

---

133.   JCT Suite of Contracts and its predecessors.

Appendix – NEC3 'Toolkit'

Communication checklist

In accordance with good project management principles, NEC3 communications are intended to cover the entire project and it is therefore no surprise that all the core clause sections include communication requirements.

The range of communications is wide and intended to be exhaustive in relation to the ability to manage a project.

The reciprocal nature of communications under NEC3 can take some practice for architects who are used to administering older style standard form contracts, where communication is a little more one way, from contract administering architect to contractor.

The following checklist is intended to give architects for whom NEC3 is a new experience a quick overview of the contractual communications which are foreseen. Most architects will find that mastering these communications is key to successful contract administration under NEC3. The checklist can also be used as an aide-memoire by relatively experienced NEC3 users. It is presented in three different orders for ease of navigation: (1) by clause number, (2) by type, and (3) by issuer.

Communication proformas

Most architects will want to prepare their own communication proformas when they are acting as Project Manager and/or Supervisor; this will allow templates to be stored for a particular project. Such templates can then include the issuer's logo and the project distribution list. Examples of the proforma types architects will become conversant with are included in this appendix (pages 89 to 100).

CHECKLIST VERSION 1 Communications ordered BY CLAUSE NUMBER

D = discretionary communication / **M** = mandatory communication

Action	Clause no.	Communication	Issued by
Notification of agreed extension to *period for reply*	13.5	Notification	Project Manager
Instruction to change Works Information or a Key Date	14.3	Instruction **D/M**	Project Manager
Notification of 'cost/time/quality' early warning matters	16.1	Notification **M**	Project Manager/ Contractor
Notification of other early warning matter	16.1	Notification **D**	Contractor
Instruction to attend risk reduction meeting	16.2	Instruction **D**	Project Manager/ Contractor
Revise Risk Register to record risk reduction meeting	16.4	Record	Project Manager
Notification of an ambiguity or inconsistency	17.1	Notification	Project Manager
Instruction to resolve the ambiguity or inconsistency	17.1	Instruction **M**	Project Manager
Notification of illegal or impossible requirements	18.1	Notification	Contractor
Instruction as to how to deal with prevention event	19.1	Instruction	Project Manager
Instruction to remove an employee	24.2	Instruction	Project Manager
Acceptance of Subcontractor	26.2	Acceptance	Project Manager
Acceptance of Subcontract	26.3	Acceptance	Project Manager
Completion Certificate	30.2	Certificate	Project Manager
Acceptance of programme	31.3	Acceptance	Project Manager
Notification of non-acceptance of programme	31.3	Notification	Project Manager

Action	Clause no.	Communication	Issued by
Instruction to stop or not to start work	34.1	Instruction	Project Manager
Take over Certificate	35.3	Certificate	Project Manager
Instruction to submit quotation for acceleration	36.1	Instruction	Project Manager
Instruction to search for defects	42.1	Instruction	Supervisor
Notification of defects	42.2	Notification	Supervisor
Defects Certificate	43.3	Certificate	Supervisor
Notification of extension to defects correction period	43.4	Notification	Project Manager
Acceptance of quotation to accommodate defect	44.2	Acceptance	Project Manager
Instruction to change Works Information, Prices and Completion Date	44.2	Instruction	Project Manager
Assessment of amount of money due	50.1	Assessment	Project Manager
Payment Certificate	51.1	Certificate	Project Manager
Notification of compensation event	61.1	Notification	Project Manager
Instruction to submit quotation for compensation event	61.1	Instruction	Project Manager
Instruction to submit quotation for proposed instruction	61.2	Instruction	Project Manager
Notification of failure to give early warning	61.5	Notification	Project Manager
Notification of correcting compensation event assumption	61.6	Notification	Project Manager
Instruction to submit alternative quotations	62.1	Instruction	Project Manager
Instruction to submit a revised quotation	62.3	Instruction	Project Manager
Acceptance of a quotation	62.3	Acceptance	Project Manager

Action	Clause no.	Communication	Issued by
Notification that a quotation will not be instructed	62.3	Notification	Project Manager
Notification of Project Manager's own assessment	62.3	Notification	Project Manager
Notification of extension of quotation period	62.5	Notification	Project Manager
Notification of Project Manager's assessment of compensation event	64.3	Notification	Project Manager
Instruction to deal with objects of value/historic interest	73.1	Instruction	Project Manager
Acceptance of insurance details	85.1	Acceptance	Project Manager
Termination Certificate	90.1	Certificate	Project Manager
Termination Payment Certificate	90.4	Certificate	Project Manager
Notification of default	91.2/.3	Notification	Project Manager

CHECKLIST VERSION 2   Communications ordered BY TYPE

D = discretionary communication / **M** = mandatory communication

Action	Communication	Issued By	Clause no.
Acceptance of Subcontractor	Acceptance	Project Manager	26.2
Acceptance of Subcontract	Acceptance	Project Manager	26.3
Acceptance of programme	Acceptance	Project Manager	31.3
Acceptance of quotation to accommodate defect	Acceptance	Project Manager	44.2
Acceptance of a quotation	Acceptance	Project Manager	62.3
Acceptance of insurance details	Acceptance	Project Manager	85.1
Assessment of amount of money due	Assessment	Project Manager	50.1
Completion Certificate	Certificate	Project Manager	30.2
Take over Certificate	Certificate	Project Manager	35.3
Defects Certificate	Certificate	Supervisor	43.3
Payment Certificate	Certificate	Project Manager	51.1
Termination Certificate	Certificate	Project Manager	90.1
Termination Payment Certificate	Certificate	Project Manager	90.4
Instruction as to how to deal with prevention event	Instruction	Project Manager	19.1
Instruction to remove an employee	Instruction	Project Manager	24.2
Instruction to stop or not to start work	Instruction	Project Manager	34.1
Instruction to submit quotation for acceleration	Instruction	Project Manager	36.1
Instruction to search for defects	Instruction	Supervisor	42.1
Instruction to change Works Information, Prices and Completion Date	Instruction	Project Manager	44.2

Action	Communication	Issued By	Clause no.
Instruction to submit quotation for compensation event	Instruction	Project Manager	61.1
Instruction to submit quotation for proposed instruction	Instruction	Project Manager	61.2
Instruction to submit alternative quotations	Instruction	Project Manager	62.1
Instruction to submit a revised quotation	Instruction	Project Manager	62.3
Instruction to deal with objects of value/historic interest	Instruction	Project Manager	73.1
Instruction to attend risk reduction meeting	Instruction **D**	Project Manager/ Contractor	16.2
Instruction to change Works Information or a Key Date	Instruction **D/M**	Project Manager	14.3
Instruction to resolve the ambiguity or inconsistency	Instruction **M**	Project Manager	17.1
Notification of agreed extension to *period for reply*	Notification	Project Manager	13.5
Notification of an ambiguity or inconsistency	Notification	Project Manager	17.1
Notification of illegal or impossible requirements	Notification	Contractor	18.1
Notification of non-acceptance of programme	Notification	Project Manager	31.3
Notification of defects	Notification	Supervisor	42.2
Notification of extension to defects correction period	Notification	Project Manager	43.4
Notification of compensation event	Notification	Project Manager	61.1
Notification of failure to give early warning	Notification	Project Manager	61.5
Notification of correcting compensation event assumption	Notification	Project Manager	61.6

Action	Communication	Issued By	Clause no.
Notification that a quotation will not be instructed	Notification	Project Manager	62.3
Notification of Project Manager's own assessment	Notification	Project Manager	62.3
Notification of extension of quotation period	Notification	Project Manager	62.5
Notification of Project Manager's assessment of compensation event	Notification	Project Manager	64.3
Notification of default	Notification	Project Manager	91.2/.3
Notification of other early warning matter	Notification **D**	Contractor	16.1
Notification of 'cost/time/quality' early warning matters	Notification **M**	Project Manager/ Contractor	16.1
Revise Risk Register to record risk reduction meeting	Record	Project Manager	16.4

CHECKLIST VERSION 3   Communications ordered BY ISSUER

D = discretionary communication / **M** = mandatory communication

Action	Issued By	Clause no.	Communication
Notification of other early warning matter	Contractor	16.1	Notification **D**
Notification of illegal or impossible requirements	Contractor	18.1	Notification
Notification of 'cost/time/quality' early warning matters	Project Manager/ Contractor	16.1	Notification **M**
Instruction to attend risk reduction meeting	Project Manager/ Contractor	16.2	Instruction **D**
Notification of agreed extension to *period for reply*	Project Manager	13.5	Notification
Instruction to change Works Information or a Key Date	Project Manager	14.3	Instruction **D/M**
Revise Risk Register to record risk reduction meeting	Project Manager	16.4	Record
Notification of an ambiguity or inconsistency	Project Manager	17.1	Notification
Instruction to resolve the ambiguity or inconsistency	Project Manager	17.1	Instruction **M**
Instruction as to how to deal with prevention event	Project Manager	19.1	Instruction
Instruction to remove an employee	Project Manager	24.2	Instruction
Acceptance of Subcontractor	Project Manager	26.2	Acceptance
Acceptance of Subcontract	Project Manager	26.3	Acceptance
Completion Certificate	Project Manager	30.2	Certificate
Acceptance of programme	Project Manager	31.3	Acceptance
Notification of non-acceptance of programme	Project Manager	31.3	Notification

Action	Issued By	Clause no.	Communication
Instruction to stop or not to start work	Project Manager	34.1	Instruction
Take over Certificate	Project Manager	35.3	Certificate
Instruction to submit quotation for acceleration	Project Manager	36.1	Instruction
Notification of extension to defects correction period	Project Manager	43.4	Notification
Acceptance of quotation to accommodate defect	Project Manager	44.2	Acceptance
Instruction to change Works Information, Prices and Completion Date	Project Manager	44.2	Instruction
Assessment of amount of money due	Project Manager	50.1	Assessment
Payment Certificate	Project Manager	51.1	Certificate
Notification of compensation event	Project Manager	61.1	Notification
Instruction to submit quotation for compensation event	Project Manager	61.1	Instruction
Instruction to submit quotation for proposed instruction	Project Manager	61.2	Instruction
Notification of failure to give early warning	Project Manager	61.5	Notification
Notification of correcting compensation event assumption	Project Manager	61.6	Notification
Instruction to submit alternative quotations	Project Manager	62.1	Instruction
Instruction to submit a revised quotation	Project Manager	62.3	Instruction
Acceptance of a quotation	Project Manager	62.3	Acceptance
Notification that a quotation will not be instructed	Project Manager	62.3	Notification
Notification of Project Manager's own assessment	Project Manager	62.3	Notification

Action	Issued By	Clause no.	Communication
Notification of extension of quotation period	Project Manager	62.5	Notification
Notification of Project Manager's assessment of compensation event	Project Manager	64.3	Notification
Instruction to deal with objects of value/historic interest	Project Manager	73.1	Instruction
Acceptance of insurance details	Project Manager	85.1	Acceptance
Termination Certificate	Project Manager	90.1	Certificate
Termination Payment Certificate	Project Manager	90.4	Certificate
Notification of default	Project Manager	91.2/.3	Notification
Instruction to search for defects	Supervisor	42.1	Instruction
Notification of defects	Supervisor	42.2	Notification
Defects Certificate	Supervisor	43.3	Certificate

Communication proformas

nec3

Project Manager's Assessment

Project:	*Paradise Found*
Employer:	*Best Practice Developments Ltd*
Contractor:	*Efficient Build Ltd*
Contract Dated:	*13.01.2013*
Issued by:	*PM Critical Path LLP*
Issue Date:	*01.06.2013*
Assessment No.:	*01*

Assessment under Clause 50.1 Amount due	Currency (£)
Price for Work Done to Date (PWDD)	*XX*
plus other amounts to be paid to the *Contractor*	*XX*
less amounts to be paid by or retained from the *Contractor*	*XX*
Any tax which the law requires the *Employer* to pay to the *Contractor*	*XX*
Total amount due	*Currency XX*
Signed on behalf of *Project Manager*	....

Copies to:

Contractor -	*Efficient Build Ltd*
Employer -	*Best Practice Developments Ltd*
Supervisor -	*QA Consulting LLP*
Structural Engineer -	*Key Performance Ltd*
M&E Consultant -	*PV Array Ltd* *etc.*

Job No. xx / PMAss xx   Page 1 of X

nec3

Project Manager's Payment Certificate

Project: *Paradise Found*

Employer: *Best Practice Developments Ltd*

Contractor: *Efficient Build Ltd*

Contract Dated: *13.01.2013*

Issued by: *PM Critical Path LLP*

Issue Date: *01.06.2013*

Payment Certificate No.:   *10*

Certificate under Clause 51.1 Payment	Currency (£)
Amount due	*XX*
less amounts previously certified	*XX*
Change in the amount due which is certified for payment	*Currency XX*
Signed on behalf of *Project Manager*	....

Copies to:

Contractor -   *Efficient Build Ltd*

Employer -   *Best Practice Developments Ltd*

Supervisor -   *QA Consulting LLP*

Structural Engineer -   *Key Performance Ltd*

M&E Consultant -   *PV Array Ltd*   *etc.*

Job No. xx / PMPC xx   Page 1 of X

nec3

Project Manager's Instruction

Project:	*Paradise Found*
Employer:	*Best Practice Developments Ltd*
Contractor:	*Efficient Build Ltd*
Contract Dated:	*13.01.2013*
Issued by:	*PM Critical Path LLP*
Issue Date:	*01.06.2013*
PMI No.:	*01*

Instruction under Clause XX

XX

XX

Signed on behalf of *Project Manager*

....

Copies to:

Contractor -	*Efficient Build Ltd*
Employer -	*Best Practice Developments Ltd*
Supervisor -	*QA Consulting LLP*
Structural Engineer -	*Key Performance Ltd*
M&E Consultant -	*PV Array Ltd*	*etc.*

Job No. xx / PMI xx   Page 1 of X

nec3

Project Manager's Instruction

Project:	*Paradise Found*
Employer:	*Best Practice Developments Ltd*
Contractor:	*Efficient Build Ltd*
Contract Dated:	*13.01.2013*
Issued by:	*PM Critical Path LLP*
Issue Date:	*01.06.2013*
PMI No.:	*02*

Instruction under Clause 14.3 Change to Works Information	Quotation No.	Completion Date	ADD £	OMIT £
XX	*XX*	*xx.xx.xx*	*XX*	*XX*
Running final cost			£	
Signed on behalf of *Project Manager*	....			

Copies to:

Contractor -	*Efficient Build Ltd*
Employer -	*Best Practice Developments Ltd*
Supervisor -	*QA Consulting LLP*
Structural Engineer -	*Key Performance Ltd*
M&E Consultant -	*PV Array Ltd* *etc.*

Job No. xx / PMI xx   Page 1 of X

nec3

Project Manager's Acceptance

Project:	*Paradise Found*
Employer:	*Best Practice Developments Ltd*
Contractor:	*Efficient Build Ltd*
Contract Dated:	*13.01.2013*
Issued by:	*PM Critical Path LLP*
Issue Date:	*01.06.2013*
Contractor's Notification No.:	*01*

Acceptance under Clause *XX*

XX

XX

Signed on behalf of *Project Manager*

....

Copies to:

Contractor -	*Efficient Build Ltd*
Employer -	*Best Practice Developments Ltd*
Supervisor -	*QA Consulting LLP*
Structural Engineer -	*Key Performance Ltd*
M&E Consultant -	*PV Array Ltd*　　　　　　　　*etc.*

Job No. xx / PMAcc xx

Page 1 of X

nec3

Project Manager's Notification

Project:	*Paradise Found*
Employer:	*Best Practice Developments Ltd*
Contractor:	*Efficient Build Ltd*
Contract Dated:	*13.01.2013*
Issued by:	*PM Critical Path LLP*
Issue Date:	*01.06.2013*
Contractor's Notification No.:	*01*

Notification under Clause *XX*

XX

XX

Signed on behalf of *Project Manager*

....

Copies to:

Contractor -	*Efficient Build Ltd*
Employer -	*Best Practice Developments Ltd*
Supervisor -	*QA Consulting LLP*
Structural Engineer -	*Key Performance Ltd*
M&E Consultant -	*PV Array Ltd* *etc.*

Job No. xx / PMN xx

Page 1 of X

nec3

Project Manager's Record of Revision to Risk Register

Project: *Paradise Found*

Employer: *Best Practice Developments Ltd*

Contractor: *Efficient Build Ltd*

Contract Dated: *13.01.2013*

Issued by: *PM Critical Path LLP*

Issue Date: *01.06.2013*

Project Manager's Record No.: *01*

Record under Clause 16.4

Risk Register

The following decisions made at the risk reduction meeting held on *XX* are recorded:

XX

XX

XX

XX

XX

and the revised Risk Register dated *XX* is issued to the Contractor with this record.

Signed on behalf of *Project Manager*	....

Copies to:

Contractor -   *Efficient Build Ltd*

Employer -   *Best Practice Developments Ltd*

Supervisor -   *QA Consulting LLP*

Structural Engineer -   *Key Performance Ltd*

M&E Consultant -   *PV Array Ltd*   *etc.*

Job No. xx / PMR xx   Page 1 of X

nec3

Project Manager's Take over Certificate

Project:	*Paradise Found*
Employer:	*Best Practice Developments Ltd*
Contractor:	*Efficient Build Ltd*
Contract Dated:	*13.01.2013*
Issued by:	*PM Critical Path LLP*
Issue Date:	*01.06.2013*
Certificate No.:	*01*

Take over under Clause 35.3	
Take over	**DATE**
The date of take over of *XX* of the *works* by the *Employer* is	*XX*
The date of take over of *YY* of the *works* by the *Employer* is	*XX*
The date of take over of *ZZ* of the *works* by the *Employer* is	*XX*
Signed on behalf of *Project Manager*	....

Copies to:

Contractor -	*Efficient Build Ltd*
Employer -	*Best Practice Developments Ltd*
Supervisor -	*QA Consulting LLP*
Structural Engineer -	*Key Performance Ltd*
M&E Consultant -	*PV Array Ltd* *etc.*

Job No. xx / PMC xx   Page 1 of X

nec3

Project Manager's Completion Certificate

Project:	*Paradise Found*
Employer:	*Best Practice Developments Ltd*
Contractor:	*Efficient Build Ltd*
Contract Dated:	*13.01.2013*
Issued by:	*PM Critical Path LLP*
Issue Date:	*01.06.2013*
Certificate No.:	*01*

Certification under Clause 30.1 Completion	DATE
if Sectional Completion (secondary option X5) applies:	
The date of Completion of *section XX* of the *works* is	*XX*
Otherwise:	
The date of Completion of the whole of the *works* is	*XX*
Signed on behalf of *Project Manager*	....

Copies to:

Contractor -	*Efficient Build Ltd*
Employer -	*Best Practice Developments Ltd*
Supervisor -	*QA Consulting LLP*
Structural Engineer -	*Key Performance Ltd*
M&E Consultant -	*PV Array Ltd* *etc.*

Job No. xx / PMC xx

Page 1 of X

nec3

Supervisor's Instruction

Project:	*Paradise Found*
Employer:	*Best Practice Developments Ltd*
Contractor:	*Efficient Build Ltd*
Contract Dated:	*13.01.2013*
Issued by:	*Supervisor QA Consulting LLP*
Issue Date:	*01.06.2013*
SI No.:	*01*

Instruction under Clause 42.1

Search for a Defect

XX

Signed on behalf of *Supervisor*

....

Copies to:

Contractor -	*Efficient Build Ltd*
Employer -	*Best Practice Developments Ltd*
Project Manager -	*Critical Path LLP*
Structural Engineer -	*Key Performance Ltd*
M&E Consultant -	*PV Array Ltd* *etc.*

Job No. xx / SI xx   Page 1 of X

nec3

Supervisor's Defects Certificate

Project: *Paradise Found*

Employer: *Best Practice Developments Ltd*

Contractor: *Efficient Build Ltd*

Contract Dated: *13.01.2013*

Issued by: *Supervisor QA Consulting LLP*

Issue Date: *01.06.2013*

SI No.: *01*

Certificate under Clause 43.3, as defined under clause 11.2(6)

Defects

XX

Signed on behalf of *Supervisor*

....

Copies to:

Contractor -   *Efficient Build Ltd*

Employer -   *Best Practice Developments Ltd*

Project Manager -   *Critical Path LLP*

Structural Engineer -   *Key Performance Ltd*

M&E Consultant -   *PV Array Ltd*   *etc.*

Job No. xx / SDC xx   Page 1 of X

nec3

Contractor's Notification

Project: *Paradise Found*

Employer: *Best Practice Developments Ltd*

Contractor: *Efficient Build Ltd*

Contract Dated: *13.01.2013*

Issued by: *Contractor Efficient Build Ltd*

Issue Date: *01.06.2013*

Contractor's Notification No.:   *01*

Notification under Clause 16.1
Early Warning
XX

Signed on behalf of *Contractor*	....

Copies to:

Employer -   *Best Practice Developments Ltd*

Project Manager   *Critical Path LLP*

Supervisor -   *QA Consulting LLP*

Structural Engineer -   *Key Performance Ltd*

M&E Consultant -   *PV Array Ltd*   *etc.*

Job No. xx / CN xx   Page 1 of X

Index